The attack of the unexpected

Magnus Lindkvist is a trendspotter based in Stockholm, Sweden. He helps companies make sense (and money) out of the future, and unexpectedly met his wife Vesna on a blind date in 2004.

The attack of the unexpected

A guide to surprises and uncertainty

Magnus Lindkvist

 **Marshall Cavendish**
Business

Copyright © 2011 Magnus Lindkvist

First published in 2011 by Marshall Cavendish Business
An imprint of Marshall Cavendish International
PO Box 65829
London EC1P 1NY
United Kingdom
info@marshallcavendish.co.uk

and

1 New Industrial Road
Singapore 536196
genrefsales@sg.marshallcavendish.com
www.marshallcavendish.com/genref

Marshall Cavendish is a trademark of Times Publishing Limited

Other Marshall Cavendish offices:
Marshall Cavendish International (Asia) Private Limited, 1 New Industrial Road, Singapore
536196 • Marshall Cavendish Corporation, 99 White Plains Road, Tarrytown NY 10591-9001,
USA • Marshall Cavendish International (Thailand) Co Ltd. 253 Asoke, 12th Floor, Sukhumvit
21 Road, Klongtoey Nua, Wattana, Bangkok 10110, Thailand • Marshall Cavendish (Malaysia)
Sdn Bhd, Times Subang, Lot 46, Subang Hi-Tech Industrial Park, Batu Tiga, 40000 Shah
Alam, Selangor Darul Ehsan, Malaysia

The right of Magnus Lindkvist to be identified as the editor of this work has been asserted by
him in accordance with the Copyright, Designs and Patents Act 1988.

A CIP record for this book is available from the British Library

ISBN 978-981-430-259-3

Cover art by Opal Works Co. Ltd

Printed and bound in Great Britain by CPI William Clowes

To anyone who will ever be attacked
by the unexpected

Contents

Prologue:
The end is the beginning

Victoria Falls, Zimbabwe. New Year's Eve, 1999. The ghostly blue swimming-pool lights cast weird, wobbly shadows on the surrounding buildings. The night is dark and the area around the pool is tranquil. The silence is deceptive. This five-star hotel is the site of several New Year's parties this evening. The one I'm attending is hosted by a friend who recently got married on Mount Bila in southern Zimbabwe. All the wedding guests spent a few weeks travelling around with the newlyweds. A kind of collective honeymoon, if you will. It is now a few hours before midnight and I have retreated to be with my own thoughts for a while, a New Year's ritual since I was very young. I dangle my feet into the cool, crisp, chlorinated water and reflect upon this mythical date. A year, a decade, a century and a millennium are drawing to a close. In the past few months, the world has been on edge – by 1990s standards, anyway – because of rampant speculation regarding the Y2K bug that would cause all computers to crash on this fateful evening because of a programming error. But since Sydney, Beijing and Mumbai have already passed midnight without any computers going haywire, Y2K is forever doomed to the "great mispredictions" chapter.

What lies ahead, I ask myself as an unseasonably chilling breeze blows in over the pool area. The torches lit along the path to the hotel restaurant flicker. The future looks bright. Dot.com companies have taken over stock markets, if not the world just yet. Most of my classmates from university have joined one and are making millions in fantasy money as their stock options soar. Many other industries are reporting record profits and double-digit growth. The world itself seems a bright place. The last few conflicts of the twentieth century seem to have ended. Russia is a democracy. America, the world's policeman. Run by an adulterer. Books with titles like *The End of History* are being published. This New Year feels less like the end of an era than the beginning of something new and hopeful.

I sigh.

The breeze has made the pool area rather cold so I get up and walk slowly back to the restaurant on the torchlit path.

The past is ending.

The future is about to begin.

Introduction:
Blindsided

"When patterns are broken, new worlds emerge"

Tuli Kupferberg

◖◗ The decade from hell

The future began with a bang, not with a whimper. The dot.com-heavy NASDAQ would peak on 10 March 2000, only to collapse the next day and begin a long slide into oblivion. Companies went bust as venture capital dried up. This recession was nothing compared to the one that would follow in 2008. A debt-ridden financial market crashed and took some of Wall Street's oldest banks with it just a few streets away from where a new kind of terrorism had shown its ugly face one September morning a few years earlier.

Where terrorism had once been an efficient yet restrictive political weapon, it had now become an assassin's tool, taking aim at anyone standing in its way – innocent men, women and children. It served as a trigger for what can best be described as World War III, although it became better known as the War on Terror. The theatres of war were Lower Manhattan and European train stations. The new Verdun and Dresden could be found in Iraq, Somalia and Afghanistan.

The seemingly straight path towards a global league of liberal democracies had been a premature vision, even

a mirage. Russia elected Vladimir Putin as its president
and became something completely different from the US-
style liberal democracy previously envisioned. China and
Middle Eastern states became the Atlas of the world as
their sovereign wealth funds propped up American and
European economies.

Religion, believed to be on the wane in the late twentieth century, came back with a vengeance and dominated everything from political debates to bestseller lists.
Even the editor of the usually carefully worded *Economist*
magazine proclaimed, "God is Back!"

Where megabytes and broadband had seemed like
the final economic frontier in the 1990s, the noughties
brought fossilized dinosaurs and plants back to the fore-
front with the soaring price of oil reaching record highs
before collapsing and then bouncing back up again.

In the middle of this hurricane of change, we all started
to talk about the weather. This once dull subject reserved
for Swedes and Brits at a loss for more exciting things to
debate became a catalyst for Oscar-winning movies, for
global conferences, for governments and for every single
individual who had ever travelled on a jet plane or driven
any car other than the purely electric kind. We gave the
this new turbulent era names: "The age of uncertainty";
"The age of the unthinkable". *Time* magazine went so far
as to call it "The Decade from Hell".

We had been attacked. Not just by ancient beliefs,
carbon emissions, fundamentalism, hyper-terrorism and
severe financial turbulence. We had been attacked by the
Unexpected.

New world disorder

"Unexpected" became the most frequently used adjective when media outlets around the world summarized the 2000s. It became not just a word but a character in itself. As such, it played a part in virtually every major event – good or bad. From the rise of new brands and competitors – think Google or Wikipedia – to catastrophic events like the 2004 tsunami or Hurricane Katrina. If life was a play, the use of the unexpected could best be likened to a divine entity coming down in the third act to change absolutely everything that had taken place before it. A deus ex machina on steroids. Sometimes benevolent. Sometimes vicious. Always unpredictable. In its appearance and in the outcome generated. Familiar became strange. Known became unknown, and since all fear is basically a fear of the unknown, many were tempted to use this new character to scare others. Books and articles were written about how nothing could be predicted any more and that we were now doomed to eternal wandering in the dark ages, oppressed by unexpected events. One book even went so far as to refer to the unexpected as "The Black Swan" – most likely aware that black birds symbolize death.

> All fear is basically a fear of the unknown

What was scary indeed was how things that used to be safe – be it a holiday in Thailand, flying on aeroplanes, travelling on the underground or keeping your money in the bank – became something like life-or-death propositions. The ordered twentieth century had a kind of predictable dramaturgy to it, with clearly delineated villains and heroes – at least if you happened to live in the rather clumsily defined area known as "the West". This permeated our culture, creating simplistic plotlines in which the Anglo-Saxon hero – from Rocky Balboa to James Bond – always prevailed. Now the rules of the drama had changed. Think of James Bond's adventures in the twenty-first century. The villains were less obvious and so were James Bond's drive and motivation. And just what does "Quantum of Solace" actually mean?

The unexpected stirred our emotions because we live in an age hell-bent on curing and understanding everything. These new events were an inconvenient reminder that we don't know everything. You could, in fact, argue that we know very little about the world we live in and the rules

We live in an age hell-bent on curing and understanding everything

that govern its many intricacies. The question is: what do you do about that?

◖ The role and structure of this book

A famous magazine editor once claimed that one should be able to summarize any written text, however long it may be, in a sentence or two. Here goes.

This book is written as a guide to help us understand the unexpected on a deeper level, with the objective of making us accept, even embrace, uncertainty. In our own lives, in our companies and in society. It is written for the kind of curious individuals, daring executives and visionary politicians that we need in an age when old truths have been replaced by question marks. Where every day is a surprise waiting to happen.

There are two different kinds of books you can write about the unexpected. One is a horror story in which you ridicule the limitations of the human mind and, like a big bully, beat us while we are down. That has been the path taken by many authors and thinkers in the past few years. I became interested in the other kind of book you could write. As a trendspotter, I have dedicated my professional life to finding new ideas in the world around us and trying to make sense of where it all might be pointing to, in the foreseeable future and in the long run. All of a sudden, "unexpected" had become a trend in itself – from the excessive usage of the word to the events that it described. This was no time to ridicule, I thought, but rather a time for understanding. Moreover, as a believer in the art and science of prediction, I needed to reconcile two divergent ideas – that you *can* predict and that you *can't* predict. Finally, I felt that it is our duty as human beings to take things out of an oppressive darkness and bring them into the light. The spirit of curiosity is part of our heritage, from science to civilization itself. That is the underlying belief of this book.

The spirit of curiosity is part of our heritage

but you can do something!

I have written it as an investigation into the kind of unexpected events that come along and change everything – whether on a personal or a broader level. I refrain from the hyperbole of my peers who claim "more and more things are unexpected" and instead enquire what it means when we say something is unexpected and what happens to us when we face it – on a psychological level, in companies and in society in general. What conclusions can we draw from it? Is the insecurity often associated with uncertainty the only effect, or can there be positive – even helpful – effects of the unexpected?

Finally, a word about my style. Most books written about uncertainty have been dry, left-brain arguments focusing on statistics and finance. Many of them have been fine intellectual pieces, but bell curves and equations have a tendency to hide human beings behind data. This book is the right-brain guide to the unexpected, focusing on meaning, emotions and practical implications. I have made a conscious decision to distance myself from the dystopian resignation displayed by other authors and will make an effort to find the positive sides of uncertainty. You might be surprised to learn that there are many.

Five dimensions of the unexpected

The book is organized into five principal chapters, each representing a set of questions and a perspective on the unexpected – an arena, if you will.

- *Defining the unexpected*: What do we actually mean when we use the epithet "unexpected"? Like postmodernism, it's defined by what it isn't. So how can we say that some things are expected and others are not?

- *The unexpected on a personal level*: What happens to us as human beings when we are attacked by the unexpected? From the jump we experience when we are startled, to the hysterical laugh triggered by an unexpected punchline.

- *The unexpected and companies*: Companies find

themselves in uncharted waters all the time and fortunes have been made or lost because of unexpected events. How do companies deal with it and how should they deal with it to improve the outcome?

● *The unexpected in society*: Countries, institutions and beliefs are dethroned or crowned when the unexpected strikes. What happens to people on a societal level when they face improbable events and uncertainty?

● *The bad side of the unexpected*: Throughout history, people have attempted to hijack the unexpected. From shamans selling anti-earthquake elixir after the great Lisbon earthquake in 1755, triggering the Age of Enlightenment, to present-day religious zealots and charlatans claiming to see patterns in disastrous events. This chapter is the antidote.

At the end of each chapter is a gaming board. The rules for playing this game are simple. All you need is a pair of dice. The point is to score as many "Enlightenment Points" as possible by the time you reach the end of the book. Chance will play a role in this just as it does in the real world, but my hope is that the game will inspire you to change your daily routines to better accommodate the attack of unexpected things.

The fact that I was intrigued by a societal trend still doesn't really explain why I wanted to write an entire book on the subject. After all, many inspiring and puzzling phenomena have crossed my radar screen since I put the title "trendspotter" on my business card in the early 2000s. There was something deeper and darker drawing me to the subject of the unexpected. Something more personal.

◖◗ When unexpected things attack

It was a cold May night many years ago when I was vio-lently awoken in the small hours of the morning by two burglars. I had been home alone studying for an upcom-ing English exam and had left a few lights on as I went to bed. It had most likely given the opportunistic intruders the false impression that nobody was home.

I was held at knifepoint and forced to disclose the whereabouts of all the valuables in the house. There weren't many, but the burglars got away with something of incalculable value – my sense of security and inner calm. It would take a few months for my parents to deal with the insurance company, but many years for me to come to terms with what happened that night.

Everyone faces some unexpected event or another in his or her lifetime. Some good. Some considerably worse than what I had to go through. My point is not to dwell on the past and portray myself as a victim. On the contrary, I can see how this ordeal made me stronger. But it did plant a seed of doubt in me. Doubt in my own capacity to accurately predict what lies ahead of me and in my ability to control it. The unexpected has haunted me since.

This book is a not just a guide but a kind of personal exorcism to see whether I too can stop worrying and start loving the unexpected. Or at least, accept it as an inevita-ble co-player in the game of life.

Are you ready to see what happens when we are attacked by the unexpected?

Stockholm

June 2010

1 Expectations 0 – Reality 1

Defining the unexpected

◖◗ A day like no other

Can you spot at least five unexpected things in the following story?

Seven a.m. Monday morning. Your alarm clock rings. You press "snooze".

You wake a few minutes later, conscious of all the things you have to do today. Besides, morning routines are calling.

Some time later, you find yourself on your way to work. Your mobile phone rings. You're late.

The work week begins with a frightfully boring meeting hosted by that guy who loves holding meetings but is incapable of making decisions – uncannily he can be found in any office around the world.

The rest of the day passes quickly, though. You're encouraged to pursue some new projects by your boss. You reconnect with an old friend over lunch. The sun is shining.

The afternoon passes without anything particularly dramatic happening, apart from a false fire alarm. But you're used to it since it's gone off about twenty times in the past month alone.

On the way home you pick up a newspaper which you enjoy over a TV dinner consisting of chicken and rice. With nothing particularly interesting on the telly tonight, you go to bed early, read a few pages of the book that's been on your nightstand for far too long now, and with sleepiness slowly dragging your concentration away from the reading, it's easy to see why.

This would be classified as an ordinary day for most us. Nothing extraordinary, just a gentle sense of everyday-ness. Nothing described above could be classified as "unexpected", right? Or?

Think of the many things that *nearly* happened that day. You nearly overslept. This might have lost you your job. Or you might have run into somebody on the way to work that you would otherwise have missed.

The old friend might have been seconds from telling you a dark secret but was cut off by something.

This might be the last false fire alarm before a real fire breaks out the following week, taking many of your colleagues' lives because nobody takes the fire alarm seriously any more.

If we re-examine what takes place in a day like this using a different mindset, we quickly deduce that most things are unexpected. Not just in terms of what nearly happened but of the events that did take place.

The exact second at which you rise from bed. The number of strokes with your toothbrush in the morning. The exact outside temperature to two decimal places. The phone calls and who they are from. The way your lunch tasted and what you and your long-lost friend talked about. And so on. What we call life is really a steady stream of random events, even chaos. But we don't refer to any of these things as unexpected. We could only imagine what our friends or spouses would say if we did and how weary of us they would become.

> What we call life is really a steady stream of random events

Every day is a potential confrontation with the unexpected, but in the majority of cases, these unexpected happenings don't interfere or interact with us, so we consider them to be mere noise, trivialities or ghosts of the mind rather than unexpected events. We reserve that epithet for certain things and in rare instances. This chapter seeks to understand when, how and why we use the word "unexpected".

so we are lucky!

◖◗ Attention is a two-way street

Human attention works like a lens through which we look out at the world. And indeed listen to it, touch it, smell it and taste it too. Of all the things that happen around us at any given moment, we focus on a minuscule portion, and when we focus, we devote top-down attention. We decide to use one or a few of our senses to examine something – from words on a page to the taste of a freshly baked bread roll. Top-down attention is also what helps us to look for our kids should they wander astray in the supermarket or when we try to find clues to unlock the next level of a computer game. In short, whenever we consciously use our five senses, top-down attention is switched on. Control is the word that best describes this kind of attention. We are firmly in the driver's seat and the world behaves more or less in the way we have come to expect. That is when its sibling sometimes makes its presence felt: bottom-up attention. We often say that something "grabs" our attention, and that is an appropriate metaphor for what happens as something yanks the shackles controlling our senses out of our hands. A strange odour slips by. Something jumps at you from behind a bush. An advertisement with sexual undertones draws your gaze away from the article or – be careful – the motorway unfolding ahead of you. Things that appear on the radar screen of bottom-up attention are what we usually refer to as unexpected. But far from all of them. We often just settle for a "that's odd", a shrug of the shoulders, and then move along the predictable path of whatever we were doing before this perceptive disturbance piqued our senses. For something to be truly unexpected, it needs to pass some other qualifying tests as well.

◖◗ The power of rarity

Statistics is the art and science of handling data, and when statisticians claim that something is unexpected, what they mean is that something is rare given expectations. Or, to put it in their words, that the outcome is far from expected. Clinical language, however, usually conceals the meaning for ordinary human beings, just as statistical death tolls hide the actual grief and suffering of those affected. Rarity does not automatically make us reach for the u-word in our vocabulary. A leap year, for instance, is relatively rare, yet it is predictable, which disqualifies it from slipping behind the velvet rope and into the "For unexpected events only" zone. The required entry qualification is that the event is not only rare in time but also in mental space. There needs to be a sense of pioneering newness surrounding the event for us to call it unexpected. Frank Knight, whose ideas once shaped our understanding of uncertainty, divided probability into three categories.[1] The first was a priori probability, whereby we know what the outcomes may be and have an idea of the frequency of each – the rolling of a die being the classic example, where each of the six numbers has a one-in-six chance of appearing. The second variety was statistical probability, whereby we start to guess the outcome based on what we have previously observed. That is how meteorologists are able to predict whether we will be wearing long johns or sandals tomorrow. Given certain known parameters like air pressure, season and winds, we know what the likely outcome will be. So far, so familiar. It is Knight's third variety we are looking for. He called it "estimates", a term to be used when "there is no valid basis of any kind for classifying instances". In other words, for events that we might never have witnessed before or even imagined possible. Rare in time. Rare in mental space.

While we are capable of great imagination, we are also magnificent at self-delusion

That is no easy feat given the human mind's impressive capacity for imagination. So just how do certain things slip through and surprise us? The answer is that while we are capable of great imagination, we are also masters of self-delusion.

◐ The lifeline

Michael Shermer has made a career out of studying why people are prone to believe weird things. As the founding editor of *Skeptic* magazine, he has written about everything from quacks to conspiracy theories. "Belief", says Shermer, "is the natural state. It's harder to be a skeptic."[2] We want to believe in a simple, cohesive narrative, whether as an explanation for catastrophes or for the meaning of life, and Shermer calls this tendency "patternicity" – the tendency to see meaningful patterns in meaningless noise.[3] One of the best examples of patternicity is the way we view our own life. Few people are prone to consider their existence as the random series of unexpected events described above, and we go to great lengths to convince ourselves that there is a master plan. We craft meticulous plans for the future and attribute our eventual success to our own actions. We talk about things like fate and serendipity as if some invisible script exists for the life we lead. We dabble in religious beliefs about an afterlife and hope that higher powers will reward our good deeds or punish the bad. Believers and sceptics alike are very reluctant to use the words "haphazard" or "meaningless" to describe their own lives. We tend to think about the days of our lives as if they are on a trajectory – let's call it the lifeline.

Our lives are connections between random events that we hope and pray will make sense

Like necklace beads on a piece of string, our lives are connections between random events that we hope and pray will make sense. When things come along that break the pattern, we react with bewilderment.

◖◗ Derailed

My friend Joe travelled with his wife to the south of France in the autumn of 2002. He was in his early forties, and had finally met the love of his life only a few years previously. They had just moved into a beautiful new house in the suburbs of Minneapolis and were making plans to have children. They were now in Cannes so she could attend a conference and they could enjoy the Riviera together. When they landed, Joe felt tired after the long flight and took a short nap in the hotel room.

He never woke up.

A burst pulmonary artery killed him.

When I met his widow a few months later at a memorial service in Manhattan, she said that her life had been derailed.

This sad story illustrates how we tend to view our lives as following a linear narrative, and when reality intervenes, we find ourselves in uncharted territory unsure of where the tracks might lead us. Or whether there were ever any tracks at all.

This is not unique to individuals. Organizations, for example, make budgets and vision statements to set out a clear path for what lies ahead. Neither is linear projection a particularly new phenomenon. On the contrary, most cultures that we know of have had some model by which to explain the trajectory of life. Perhaps the most similar one to the idea of a lifeline is the ancient Norse concept of *wyrd*[4] or fate-thread. Wyrds were spun by the Norns, three women who wove the fate of man on a spindle. The threads could be long and straight or short and tangled.

We may laugh at the superstitions of kooky Vikings today, yet the mental model of life as a linear narrative lives on. Someone once said of science that all models are wrong but some are useful, and we can apply the same logic to this mental model. It is a self-delusion – a reality distortion field – that helps us to plan ahead and view our lives as something meaningful.

S as in changes

To the dismay of psychopaths and visionaries alike, reality does not behave as we want it to and "unexpected" is the name we give reality when it collides with and contradicts our expectations. These collisions are bound to be more frequent in times of great turbulence – economic, political or technological. At any given moment, most things are stagnant. Held in place by a power equilibrium between the forces promoting change and those opposing it. Change happens either when the forces opposing it weaken or those promoting it strengthen. Depending on how quickly these forces decline or increase, change will either be slow and gradual or revolutionary. It is the latter kind which interests me in this book. Gradual change, such as ageing or evolution, is what we live with on a daily basis, and its slowness tends to make us blind to it – most of us consider ourselves to be twenty-three years old until the day we discover a nasty lump somewhere on our body or that our way of dancing isn't considered particularly hip any more. Quick change, on the other hand, surprises and disillusions us. Left-wing activist and author Naomi Klein points to the fact that quick and shocking

changes – think of Hurricane Katrina in New Orleans or
the financial collapse of Iceland – make us lose the narrative thread. We don't know what it is we are looking
at and experiencing. Innovation theorists talk about an
S-curve wherein nothing happens, then everything, just
as in the curvature of an S. Think of the Internet. Its roots
can be traced back to the 1960s but it was dormant for a
long time, finding users only among the most avid technology whizz-kids or academics. Then, with the invention of the World Wide Web and the Mosaic web browser,
use of the Internet exploded in the early 1990s. Nothing.
Then everything. The same kind of trajectory can be seen
in developments like the fall of Yugoslavia and the Soviet
Union in the early 1990s or the rise of iPods and Twitter
in the 2000s.

To put it in the words of Harvard historian Niall Ferguson: "What if history is not cyclical and slow-moving
but arrhythmic – at times almost stationary but also
capable of accelerating suddenly, like a sports car? What
if [change] does not arrive over a number of centuries but
comes suddenly, like a thief in the night?"[5]

It is in the sharp ascension of the S – which in the real
world can also be inverted and become a steep decline,
of course – that we are disoriented and marvel at the
strange, new happenings around us. What it comes down
to is that we have a sphere of expectations, like a radar
screen, where certain things are common and others are
not. This sphere is highly flexible and adaptive, however,
which is why the S-curve flattens out eventually. Markets
become saturated and political turmoil settles on some
new plateau.

◖◗ The ingredients of unpredictability

To clarify and summarize the social definition of the word "unexpected", I have developed the following formula:

$$\text{THE UNEXPECTED} = (S + M + A) \times P$$

S = *the speed with which the event described as "unexpected" occurs.* Speed, as Einstein once proved, is relative. An archaeologist and a news anchor refer to completely different things when using the words "unexpected" or "suddenly", but they both mean that the event described somehow breaks the pattern that they were expecting – whether it took millions of years or a few milliseconds.

M = *the magnitude of the event itself.* Think of the average day described in the introduction to this chapter. The reason why we don't consider the many haphazard, random events unexpected is that they are small and insignificant. The unknown stranger on the bus is meaningless from your point of view unless it turns out that he is a long-lost relative whom you thought was dead or is carrying a rucksack full of explosives and detonates it on the bus. The greater the magnitude – counted, for instance, in the number of lives touched or taken – the more unexpected we consider the event to be.

A = *the aftermath of the event.* Magnitude and aftermath are indeed related but not necessarily correlated. Two Boeing 747s nearly colliding in the skies above Heathrow has a greater magnitude than two Ford Sierras narrowly avoiding collision on the M25, but if the aircraft fly safely on to their destinations while the Fords cause the biggest highway traffic jam in history, we are certain to refer to the automotive incident as the more "unexpected" of the two.

P = preconceived notions. Finally, there is an accelerator consisting of our preconceived notions. Think of the sphere of expectations. The firing of an AK-47 is an everyday event in a war zone but would make everyone fall to the floor in shock were it to take place at your local post office on a Monday morning. Depending on where we are and when we are, our definition of what is expected changes. Furthermore, things tend to be a lot more unexpected *before* they happen – think of airline security procedures before and after September 2001, for example.

The challenge and the opportunity

News channels and doomsday prophets have used the words unexpected and unsafe interchangeably in the past decade as if an unpredictable world is automatically less secure. Are we right to fear the unexpected and make such a big fuss about it?

To an extent, the answer is yes. The peacekeeping mechanisms put in place after 1945 are terrific at preventing a war like World War II but less efficient when it comes to the asymmetrical aggression seen in places like Iraq, Afghanistan or Somalia. Speaking to members of the Swedish armed forces, I was told that having Russia as an enemy was preferable to the potential hostility Sweden faces today: "Russia was comparatively predictable. We would see them coming and they would probably even call ahead [if they were to invade Sweden]. These days, all it takes to destabilize a nation is a few individuals. That is a lot more challenging for us as an organization."[6]

Let us change the question and instead of asking whether the world is more unpredictable and where that leads us, think about where we would be without unexpected things. Think of all the things in life that are built on the unexpected. Where would gambling be without it? Or the thrill of watching a live football game? Or any novel, book, film or drama for that matter? These are things that need unpredictability in order to be engaging. Predictable, in these instances, becomes a reason to dislike and disengage.

Horror and humour are two genres that use the unexpected to generate the desired effect. Jokes are built around a turning point where the plot takes an unexpected turn and we laugh. "Horror can be very similar to comedy," says film director Sam Raimi, "the way you set up expectations and lead the audience down a path. The punch line of a joke is not that different from the punch line in a horror scene. Each results in an involuntary audible reaction."[7]

The dramatic turning points of the arts are also what make good advertising so effective. Branding expert Marty Neumeier says that "our brains act as filters to protect us from too much information [so we become] hardwired to notice only what's different".[8] Any successful advertising campaign will have succeeded in reaching through the clutter and infiltrating your brain by being different and unexpected in a world of predictable routines.

The unexpected is, in other words, a double-edged sword. One which can scare the bejeezus out of us in certain situations, frustrate us to tears in others and make us smile delightedly at other moments. The next chapter will focus on what actually happens in our brain when the unexpected attacks.

Chapter 1 – The Game

Rules: The underlying belief of this game is simple; unexpected things open your mind. Your goal is to acquire as many enlightenment points as possible while making your way through the game. All you need is a pair of dice. May the road ahead be full of surprises!

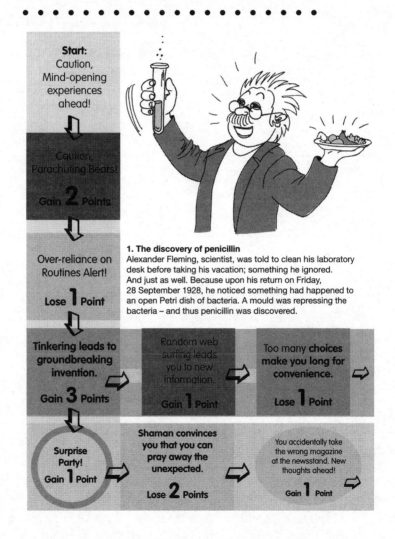

Start:
Caution,
Mind-opening
experiences
ahead!

Caution,
Parachuting Bears!

Gain **2** Points

Over-reliance on
Routines Alert!

Lose **1** Point

1. The discovery of penicillin
Alexander Fleming, scientist, was told to clean his laboratory desk before taking his vacation; something he ignored. And just as well. Because upon his return on Friday, 28 September 1928, he noticed something had happened to an open Petri dish of bacteria. A mould was repressing the bacteria – and thus penicillin was discovered.

Tinkering leads to
groundbreaking
invention.

Gain **3** Points

Random web
surfing leads
you to new
information.

Gain **1** Point

Too many **choices**
make you long for
convenience.

Lose **1** Point

**Surprise
Party!**
Gain **1** Point

Shaman convinces
you that you can
pray away the
unexpected.

Lose **2** Points

You accidentally take
the wrong magazine
at the newsstand. New
thoughts ahead!

Gain **1** Point

2 The surprised mind

What the unexpected does to the brain and the soul

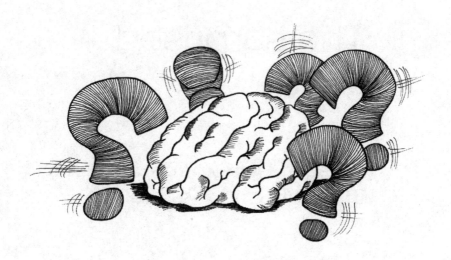

"Ah, what a dusty answer gets the soul,
When hot for certainties in this our life"

George Meredith

Getting high on surprises

It's just past lunch as the salesman, let's call him Mario, enters the sparsely furnished office for a sales call. The gentlemen he's meeting greet him with a smile and invite him to take a seat on the sofa as they both slouch down in two armchairs. Mario's shirt and tie are a stark contrast to the casual Hawaiian shirts and shorts of his potential customers, but it doesn't seem to bother him. He starts talking to them about a new offering and they listen intently. For some strange reason, the men have asked that the conversation be filmed, so sitting beside Mario is a cameraman armed with a camcorder.

Mario makes some small talk.

They laugh together.

All of a sudden:

"RAT-TAT-TAT!"

Bullets riddle the office through the window.

Two of the men are hit and shake violently before they fall on the floor in a pool of blood.

Mario frowns in panic and curls up on the sofa with his hands over his head.

His eyes are wide with terror.

His mouth is agape.

His body is frozen in a pose that is part protective, part foetal position.

The cameraman zooms in on his face. "Scream – you're on *Panic Face King*!"

It's unclear whether this famous YouTube clip is an actual Japanese TV show or the work of an amateur with a large budget. The goal of *Panic Face King* is, however, to cause its victims to display a "panic face" for the delight of a studio audience.

The reason why nasty surprises like these are so effective in causing a panic face is that our reaction is purely involuntary. Just like the little jump we experience when something startles us. Or the laughter when something funny happens before our eyes.

The question is why these involuntary reactions occur and what they mean.

The answer begins with two different processes in the brain. Imagine someone jumping out from behind a tree to scare you as you're walking in the forest. Even though it's just a close friend of yours, the initial reaction is one of complete shock and confusion, if only for a few milliseconds. Then you realize that it's just Bob and you relax, slightly annoyed perhaps by Bob's childish sense of humour.

These two reactions – panic then relaxation – aren't the result of the brain reacting to two different bits of information. It was the same Bob all along. Rather, they're the result of two different parts of the brain processing the *same* information.

The first process takes place in the area known as the reptilian brain, and is rapid and intuitive.

The second process takes place in other parts of the brain, and is slower and deliberative.

Bob jumps out to frighten us and our instinct reacts to him as a threat. Our entire system kicks into overdrive to either fight or flee.

Then we literally come to our senses to analyse the situation and recognize Bob's familiar post-mischief grin. Relief. The body produces hormones to make us relax.

A similar process takes place when we laugh at a joke. Take the following as an example:

"A couple of hunters are out in the woods when one of them falls to the ground. He doesn't seem to be breathing and his eyes are rolled back in his head.

"The other guy whips out his mobile phone and calls the emergency services. He gasps to the operator: 'My friend is dead! What can I do?'

"The operator, in a calm, soothing voice, says: 'Just take it easy. I can help. First, let's make sure he's dead.'

"There is a silence, then a shot is heard. The guy's voice comes back on the line. He says: 'OK, now what?' "[1]

This was supposedly – and rather bafflingly – voted the funniest joke in the world ever in a 2002 survey. Regardless of whether you found this particular story funny or not, theorists are in agreement that an essential ingredient in a successful joke is "an incongruity between two elements which can be resolved in a playful or unexpected way".[2] In the joke above, the incongruity is the misunderstanding between the hunter and the emergency services representative as to the meaning of the phrase "let's make sure he's dead".

Another popular approach to creating an unexpected effect in jokes is to use the number three. Take jokes based on national stereotypes as an example of this.

"An Englishman, an Irishman and a Scotsman walk into a pub together. They proceed to each buy a pint of Guinness. Just as they are about to enjoy their creamy beverage, three flies land in their pints, one in each."[3]

The first character's purpose is to establish a kind of behaviour. In this case, the Englishman pushes his beer away from him in disgust.

The second character is there to create a pattern in the behaviour. In this case, the Irishman fishes the offending fly out of his beer and continues drinking it as if nothing has happened.

The third character is the one who breaks the mould and does something unexpected.

The Scotsman picks the fly out of his drink, holds it out over the beer and then starts yelling, "Spit it out! Spit it out, you thieving bastard!"

The developments in brain-scanning techniques in the past few years have lessened mystery and opened up new doors in the understanding of how our minds work. Apart from seeing the brain's language comprehension systems work when we laugh at jokes, scientists have also discovered that jokes release a dose of dopamine in the brain. Dopamine is part of the body's reward system, which explains the pleasure we feel once we "get" a joke. We can, in other words, get high on the unexpected. This explains why some people are addicted to *South Park* and others to horror movies. Horror and humour both use unexpected

We can get high on the unexpected

resolutions to create involuntary reactions that, in turn, produce dopamine.

🌓 Why we hate the unexpected

Pleasure is certainly not the only thing we feel when facing unexpected events and uncertainty. If that were the case, people would crash cars and get divorces at random just for the sheer adrenaline rush they cause. Another common reaction is stress, shock and trauma. Post-traumatic stress disorder (PTSD for short), for example, is a syndrome affecting victims of severe emotional trauma who have experienced something unexpected that causes an intensely negative emotional reaction – a violent accident, a physical attack or encounters in a war zone are common reasons for PTSD. There is something disturbing about completely unexpected stress. Scientists have found that children delivered by Caesarean section – where the child is drastically, not gradually, exposed to the extreme emotional stress of life outside the womb – have changes in their DNA that might explain why some of them are more receptive to immunological diseases like asthma, diabetes and even cancer later in life.[4]

Intense stress seems to have an ability to reprogramme our DNA later in life too. A study conducted in China of people who had lived through the large 2008 Sichuan earthquake showed changes in the brains of these people, even if they themselves felt no trauma whatsoever.[5] Furthermore, when emotional trauma is particularly severe, it's as if the brain switches off and we are unable to form new memories. That is why eyewitness accounts during disasters and other extreme events can be so unreliable.[6]

What stressful events tend to have in common is our inability to control them, and human beings hate helplessness. A frequently quoted study called "Long-term effects of a control-relevant intervention with the institutionalized aged" showed that old people tend to become more active and feel happier and less prone to dying if they are told that they are responsible for themselves and asked to look after plants and flowers. Conversely, the patients in the studies who weren't given plants and were told that they were the responsibility of the staff became weaker and had a higher death rate. Control is an integral reason to live. Not only do elderly people seem to die from loss of control, but it also affects how we look at risks and risk-taking. Research has shown that people tend to be overconfident about risks that they can control ("I'll never die in a car crash or from lung cancer or fall to my death inside my own home"), even though these risks are a lot more prevalent than fatal accidents. What does scare us are the things we can't control, making us fear events that we are statistically unlikely to ever experience, such as a plane crash, a terrorist attack or – as can be the case in Sweden in the wintertime – being struck by a falling icicle.[7]

Human beings hate helplessness

◖◗ The veneer of sanity

To avoid the potential threat of the unexpected, we develop a set of tacit rules that we live by. In the brain, they're known as heuristics – mental models, or prejudice, to use a more common term. The word prejudice tends to have a negative connotation, however, whereas many heuristics are beneficial – it's probably wise to jump out of the way when an aggressive-looking dog approaches because nine times out of ten aggressive-looking dogs will be aggressive. When it comes to actual behaviour, we are bound by routines. "We are more automatic than we would like to think,"[8] says neurobiology professor Lars Olson of Stockholm's Karolinska University. Some of our routines are absolute – we need to eat, sleep and drink – but others are the result of brain chemistry. Habits and routines are an evolutionary protection measure against stress. If we were to deeply reflect on each and every option presented to us, it would consume a massive amount of energy and drastically increase stress levels. So we disengage a large part of the brain through living by routines – the oft-cited fact that we use only 10–20 per cent of our brain's capacity relates to the brain when it is in this comfortable, less energy-consuming routine mode.

> Habits and routines are an evolutionary protection measure against stress

One of the most potent symbols of our love for habits and routines is brands and branding. Says branding expert Don Williams: "Brands, by their very nature, are comforting; we buy them because we are reassured by their promise, because they are familiar and because they often become 'part of the family'."[9] What brands represent is uncertainty reduction. We may occasionally find ourselves in an adventurous mood ("Wow, half-price day-old sushi! I'll take all of it!"), but when we are tired of making choices and taking risks, we are thankful that there is a McDonald's at the next exit or a Heineken for sale in the hotel bar.

◖◗ Passionately pursuing weirdness

"Lonely hearts" tag-line

"Routine-seeking creatures who detest most things unexpected" would be a suitable tagline if human beings advertised in lonely-hearts columns on other planets. Even though many of us like to view ourselves as somewhat adventurous and enjoy sampling new experiences, there is a built-in filter inside our heads that prevents us from steering too far off the beaten track. It's called the anterior cingulate cortex, but is better known by its nickname, the "Oh Shit!" circuit. It is typically associated with the perception of errors and contradictions and is activated when people watch, hear and experience something that doesn't feel quite right, something that shouldn't work.[10] The circuit is, in other words, a kind of immune system intended to shelter our thoughts and sanity from savage attacks by things that don't make any sense. If we were to see rain fall upwards into the sky, the "Oh Shit!" circuit would kick into gear. We would quip, "That's weird," rub our eyes to make sure that we are seeing things accurately, and in most instances realize that it was merely an optical illusion. It wasn't reversed rainfall, it was just raindrops falling so hard on to the pavement that they bounced.

Unexpected things tend to be unexpected, however, because we have never experienced them before, so we have no concept of them before they occur. Think of the many amateur videos that appeared after the tsunami disaster in 2004. What is striking in many of them is how blasé many people seem as they stare out at sea, watching some strange-looking waves heading for shore. When we watch these videos, we want to yell, "Run, while you still can!", but we have the benefit of hindsight because we know what it is we are witnessing. Many of the tourists featured in these videos had – like many of us – never heard of a tsunami, much less grasped its destructive force. Similarly, a number of people were heard shouting things like "Holy shit!" and similar profanities when watching the Twin Towers collapse on 9/11. When eyewitnesses were being interviewed in the days following the attacks, they often repeated that what they had seen "felt unreal" and "just like in the movies".

This feeling of the unfamiliar can be frightening, but it also has a number of beneficial effects.

Opening the mind

Life is full of bad breaks and pleasant surprises, opportunities and insults. Occasionally, it also serves up things like a pink unicorn; the three-dollar bill; the nun with a beard; the "slithy toves", to borrow from the Lewis Carroll poem, that "gyre and gimble in the wabe".[11] These disorienting, weird, even creepy instances of stumbling on to the unexpected can actually train the brain into seeing new things. Things it would otherwise have missed. "We're so motivated to get rid of that feeling that we look for meaning and coherence elsewhere,"[12] says Travis Proulx, a postdoctoral researcher at the University of California; "we channel the feeling into some other project, and it appears to improve some kinds of learning." Take the following example. Imagine yourself walking down a city street when a stranger suddenly approaches and insults you, although you've done nothing to offend him. If you are like most people, your first instinct after this unpleasant experience will be to call up a friend or close relative to talk about it. The reason is not only that it is strange to be insulted for no particular reason, but also because the brain yearns to come back to coherence and meaning, which is what friends and close relatives usually provide.

Researchers have gone a step farther and confronted forest hikers with situations intended to confuse them – such as putting an armchair in the middle of the forest, as if dropped from the sky – to find them "retreat[ing] to familiar patterns like checking their equipment". They have also found evidence, however, that these situations sharpen the senses because the brain turns its attention outward, so the hikers might all of a sudden notice animal tracks that were previously hidden.[13]

In another study, students were asked to read a nonsensical, Kafkaesque short story – it was in fact written by Franz Kafka – and found that this improved the students' "implicit learning", knowledge gained without awareness. They scored almost twice as well on a pattern-recognition exercise compared with students who hadn't read the Kafka piece. This, researchers speculate, might be because of a spike of activity in the anterior cingulated cortex – the "Oh Shit!" circuit described earlier – that causes an increase in motivation to detect and correct perceptual errors in the real world. When the unexpected makes little or no sense, it may improve the way we learn about and look upon the world.

The thrill of the unknown

If the only relationship people had with the unexpected was diluted hatred – diluted because it occasionally made us perform better in lab experiments – things like roller coasters or surprise parties would make no sense. Many people, however, enjoy the adrenaline rush of a sudden drop at the funfair or the "Surprise!" chorus from a dozen friends as you switch on the lights at home. The reason, again, lies hidden in the brain. In a peculiar experiment described in the *Journal of Neuroscience*, test subjects were asked to lie down but were told nothing about what would happen next. With the subjects' heads hooked up to an MRI brain scanner, researchers then proceeded to squirt either fruit juice or water into the mouths of the subjects. The squirt patterns were either regular and predictable or completely random. The MRI scan results were surprising but give us a clue as to why we enjoy surprises. The test subjects who had fruit juice squirted into their mouths in unpredictable patterns enjoyed the fruit juice a lot more than those who had regular squirt intervals. Those experiencing the water squirts were used as a control group since the sugar and taste in fruit juice activate the brain's pleasure and reward centres.

The conclusion from the experiment is that people enjoy unpredictable pleasures – random fruit juice squirts or roller coasters – a lot more than predictable ones. This might also explain why some people become addicted to gambling, since poker, blackjack and slot machines are delivery vehicles for random bursts of pleasure and excitement.[14] A recent advertisement I spotted in a magazine summarized it rather well with the slogan "Expectation loves surprise".

◖◗ The surprise economy

Think of all the economic offerings created to generate positive surprises – from engagement rings and birthday cake ingredients to horror movie tickets. Any attempt to quantify this would run into the billions, regardless of what currency we use. We have even seen new companies built exclusively on the premise of surprise. Shirt-maker The Hipstery, for example, with the slogan "liberating you from the burden of choice", sends you a mystery shirt based on your values and opinions. Or take Japan's Kashiwa Mystery Café, where guests intentionally never get what they ordered. Apple, the creator of Mac computers, iPhones and the iPad, might be the most admired example of the past decade: *Time* magazine described their success as being based on the fact that they "never hold focus groups.

> People enjoy the thrill of surprise and the pleasure of the unexpected

Apple

They don't ask people what they want; they tell them what they're going to want next."[15] The burden of choice might in fact be an important driver of the surprise economy. Think of all the media pundits in the 1990s who believed that future news consumption would be completely tailor made and that people would ignore all kinds of advertising. Statements like these disregarded the fact that people enjoy the thrill of surprise and the pleasure of the unexpected.

The creative impulse

Per Gessle is one of Sweden's most successful musicians ever. As one half and the creative engine of the musical duo Roxette, he sold 45 million albums and had four number-one singles in the USA and the UK. In the spring of 1988 this was yet to happen. He had seen moderate success in Sweden but little or no interest abroad. Having recently purchased an Ensonic ESQ-1 synthesizer, he was now busy trying to learn how to use it.[16] Keyboards were at this time expensive pieces of machinery that often required a fair bit of technical expertise and featured thick, cumbersome instruction manuals by authors with little or no grasp of the English language. Gessle put the thick manual aside and started randomly pressing buttons on the ESQ-1. While attempting to programme the built-in sequencer, he stumbled upon a bass line made up of three chords – A, C and D. These three chords became the basis for the single "The Look", one of the most successful pop singles ever.

What Gessle's tinkering illustrates is the unpredictable

nature of creativity in general and of musical improvisation in particular. William James famously described the creative process as a "seething cauldron of ideas, where everything is fizzling and bobbing about in a state of bewildering activity".[17] If we were to hook Gessle's brain – or that of any other creative tinkerer – up to an MRI brain scanner, two things would become obvious, two clues as to what kind of brain activity the creative improvisation behind "The Look" consists of. The first is lowered activity in the areas that govern self-restraint and drive inhibitions. These are the areas of the brain that develop last in human beings, which is why we call children creative when all they're really being is uninhibited. Inhibitions and self-restraint are, after all, what we refer to as maturity. Shifting these blocks means that the thoughts are free to play around a bit more.

The second clue evident in the MRI brain scan concerns the so-called self-expression area. This area tends to be active when someone tells a story in which they themselves are the main character. Scientists argue that this area is vital for musical improvisation because "the musicians are channelling their artistic identity, searching for the notes that best summarize their style".[18] Think of Gessle again. He throws away the manual – instructive words written by someone else – and his brain disconnects certain inhibitions ("Advanced machines like the ESQ-1 need to be treated with caution and respect", for example) and invites his personality to use the synthesizer as an extension of itself.

> Inhibitions and self-restraint are what we refer to as maturity

Says *New Yorker* journalist Louis Menand on how the brain creates: "The mind is a fabulator. It is designed (by natural selection, if you like) to dream up ideas and experiences away from the mean. Its overriding instinct is to be counter-instinctual … [That] is why we have the 'Guinness Book of World Records,' the Gautama Buddha, and The Museum of Modern Art. They represent the repudiation of the norm."[19] Creativity, from a neurological perspective, is an epiphany of the unexpected.

> **Creativity is an epiphany of the unexpected**

◖◗ Forever young

As people grow older, they tend to use the phrase "time flies" or a variation thereof to describe anything from memories of youth to the latest summer vacation. This was hardly the way we described a summer holiday or a school year as we were growing up. Back then, a year was an eternity and the time before and after a holiday would feel like two different lives. What happened? The scientific theory behind this phenomenon is that "when you experience something for the very first time, more details, more information gets stored in your memory".[20]

Think about the first time you kissed someone, and compare the vividness of that memory with the eighty-sixth time it happened. When Madonna sings about being "touched for the very first time", she may well be referring to a new experience touching new parts of the senses and memory banks. With age, the number of novel experiences decreases. We settle into routines and have gained all kinds of life experience. Most things become fairly predictable and the thrill of the unknown becomes rare. Neuroscientist David Eagleman argues: "the more memory you have of something, [the longer it seems to have lasted] ... I know when I look back on a childhood summer, it seems to have lasted forever".[21]

This might explain why so many older empty-nesters strap on the backpack and head off for Vietnam and Machu Picchu nowadays; they simply want to relive the rush of a new experience. This might not only help in slowing down time. It may also refresh the mind and move it in new directions. One of the regret-table facts of life is that our ability to obtain and store new information lessens with age. Deborah M. Burke, profes-sor of psychology at Pomona College in California, has found that "neural connections, which receive, process and transmit information, can weaken with disuse or age".[22] This is why we more easily forget things like names, books we've read or errands as we grow older. The antidote is to "nudge neurons in the right direction ... to challenge the very assumptions they have worked so hard to accu-mulate while young".[23] In other words, to expose yourself to new thoughts and ideas that run contrary to what you have come to believe. "If you always hang around with those you agree with and read things that agree with what you already know, you're not going to wrestle with your established brain connections,"[24] says Professor Kathleen Taylor.

The mystique of the unexpected – whether in the shape

> The mystique of the unexpected is like anti-ageing cream for the soul

of a new experience or a new thought – is like anti-ageing cream for the soul.

◖◗ The blessed curse

We fear and loathe the unexpected, yet it also leads to wisdom, creative genius and a more meaningful life. This is not unlike physical exercise.

Imagine if we had no knowledge of what running, walking or weightlifting did inside our bodies and only had our own reaction to go on. We would probably draw the conclusion that these activities were bad for us. They make us short of breath, sweat and get feverishly warm, and quite often we have a severe ache in muscles and tendons the day after. Surely something so unpleasant cannot be good for us. Yet exercise has proved to be something of a miracle elixir. It can prevent diseases, improve wellbeing, focus our minds and help us lead better lives.

Similarly, unexpected events can cause pain and heartache. They can shake our worldview to the foundations and make us disillusioned. These effects can be felt for years, sometimes for the rest of our lives. Yet unexpected events are what drive us. From the delightful joke and the fright of a well-made thriller to the pleasures of creativity and discovery. The unexpected might indeed function like exercise for the soul and might one day be prescribed as a preventive treatment for elderly people and authors suffering from writer's block in the same way that physical exercise is an imperative in today's society.

With those words, we zoom out of our heads and focus on what happens when the unexpected meets the people who gather in groups to solve problems and address customer needs in order to make some money – better known as the corporate world.

Chapter 2 – The Game

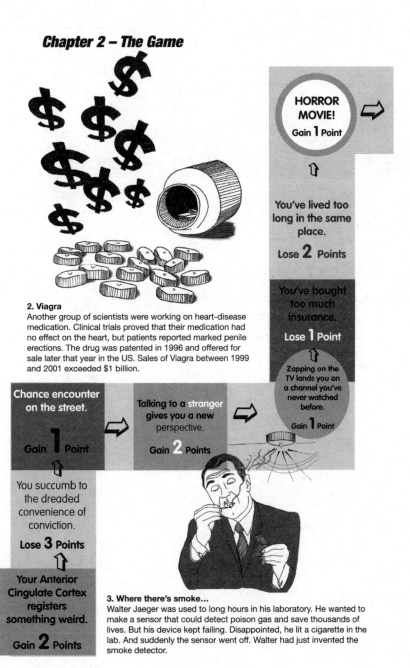

HORROR MOVIE!

Gain **1** Point

You've lived too long in the same place.

Lose **2** Points

You've bought too much insurance.

Lose **1** Point

Zapping on the TV lands you on a channel you've never watched before.

Gain **1** Point

2. Viagra

Another group of scientists were working on heart-disease medication. Clinical trials proved that their medication had no effect on the heart, but patients reported marked penile erections. The drug was patented in 1996 and offered for sale later that year in the US. Sales of Viagra between 1999 and 2001 exceeded $1 billion.

Chance encounter on the street.

Gain **1** Point

Talking to a stranger gives you a new perspective.

Gain **2** Points

You succumb to the dreaded convenience of conviction.

Lose **3** Points

Your Anterior Cingulate Cortex registers something weird.

Gain **2** Points

3. Where there's smoke…

Walter Jaeger was used to long hours in his laboratory. He wanted to make a sensor that could detect poison gas and save thousands of lives. But his device kept failing. Disappointed, he lit a cigarette in the lab. And suddenly the sensor went off. Walter had just invented the smoke detector.

3 Corporate turbulence

How companies thrive and fail unexpectedly

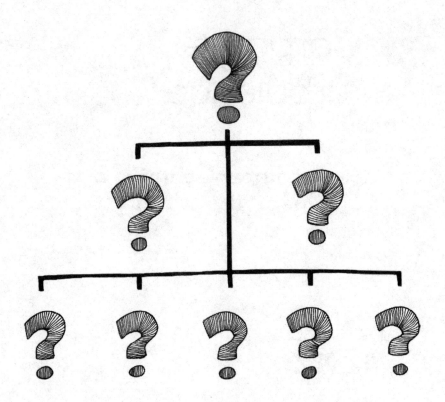

◖◗ Change animals

In a 2010 survey by IBM of over 1,500 CEOs worldwide, two words crop up repeatedly: complexity and uncertainty. This has been "the new normal" for companies around the world for the past decade. Where markets were once local, stable and predictable, they are increasingly volatile, complex and subject to competition from the most unlikely places. Deloitte's Centre for the Edge showed that asset-wide profitability has decreased for US firms from an average of just over 4.5 per cent in the mid-1960s to less than 0.5 per cent in the 2000s.[1] The story is repeated in Europe, where national monopolies and industry captains have fallen prey to globalized markets and complacency. Some people doubtless yearn for the past, when profits were easy and the future was certain. Others adapt to a new era where business must constantly take uncertainty into account. "There isn't the luxury of time. We used to say, 'Wait until this crisis is over and we get back to normal,' but that never happens. We have to be 'change animals,'"[2] to quote an executive interviewed in the IBM survey. This chapter will look at uncertainty as a part of everyday life for a corporation, and its many unexpected upsides. We will begin with the lifeblood of organizations, innovation.

Business must constantly take uncertainty into account

◖◗ The spark

Lars liked football. When he wasn't working at his day job as a salesman for a medical company, he could be found on some nearby pitch in the suburbs of Stockholm kicking a ball around with some close friends. Then, in the autumn of 1984, he was headhunted to become the CEO of a small medical company based in Gothenburg, and thus forced to leave his beloved hobby behind. Moving to a new town, as anyone who has done it can attest, can be a lonely endeavour, and for Lars it was no different. To combat the loneliness and find some physical activity to replace football, he started jogging. A lot.

The medical company that Lars was now heading specialized in products for colostomy patients – people who have had part of their colon removed and replaced by a plastic bag. As you can imagine, colostomy surgery is stigmatizing, so it is imperative that the plastic bag be discreet and comfortable. For many years, it wasn't even a plastic bag but a metal box that had to be rinsed out a number of times per day. Then disposable bags came along and another issue had to be addressed: how to make the bags stay in place while on the patient. This was solved using a thick, gooey and sticky substance, which in turn caused patients great discomfort in the form of rashes and blisters. That's where Lars's company came in. They had patented a new kind of padded adhesive tape that absorbed moisture and enabled the skin to breathe – a solution that offered much greater comfort for the patients.

Lars's frequent running made his feet suffer. With jogging shoes in the early 1980s being less sophisticated than they are today, he quickly suffered nasty blisters. Unwilling to give up his newfound passion, and being someone who enjoyed tinkering, he started thinking of a solution to help his feet recover. One afternoon, as he was sitting alone in his apartment, he took a few of the adhesive pads for colostomy bags and cut them into a shape that would suit his heel – the area with the worst blisters. He went out for a run and was able to complete his usual route without his feet causing him any trouble. Giddy with delight, he returned home and started developing his new idea. Sitting next to a military doctor while on a train to Stockholm a few weeks later, he told him about the idea and together they decided to test it on some soldiers who were scheduled for a ten-mile march the following week. The results were stunning. The control group – who had worn nothing but socks underneath their heavy leather boots – complained of foot-ache and blisters. The soldiers who had worn Lars's tape were fine, and claimed it was their best march ever.

Lars had stumbled upon something remarkable. A simple solution to a common everyday problem.

The rest is history.

The company started selling Compeed™ pads to prevent blisters on feet, elbows, hands and fingers in 1985, and the product grew to become one of the most successful medical brands ever. As Lars says today: "The greatest joy I get from this is when I and my children are travelling to some remote and exotic place and I'm able to find and show them Compeed™ being sold in the local pharmacy – this idea that started with me tinkering by myself in my little Gothenburg apartment."[3]

Unexpected business opportunities

What the story of Lars and Compeed™ serves to illustrate is the somewhat mysterious origin of successful business ideas. Companies spend billions on research and development, only to find that groundbreaking new products and solutions come about by accident. To quote the novelist Samuel Butler: "All the inventions that the world contains, were not by reason first found out, nor brain; but pass for theirs who had the luck to light upon them by mistake or oversight."[4]

The late Peter Drucker – nicknamed the management gurus' guru – even claimed that one of the most effective sources of innovation was the unexpected. There were three types, he argued: unexpected success, unexpected failure and an unexpected outside event. "The unexpected is a symptom," claimed Drucker, "but a symptom of what? The underlying phenomenon may be nothing more than a limitation on our own vision, knowledge, and understanding."[5] The challenge, he argued, was to quickly recognize what it was you were looking at and make it grow instead of fighting it – to make the unexpected your business ally, in essence.

The corporate story

Invention is an arcane, even messy, endeavour. Running a business day to day, on the other hand, is a matter of clarity. Knowing what needs to be done, by whom, when and where. Business writer Joan Magretta likens a business model to a story that explains how an enterprise works. A good business model – like a good story – should have "precisely delineated characters, plausible motivations and a plot that turns on an insight about value".[6] Think of the similarities between the way businesses and the mind work. Just as we define life as being on a linear trajectory, companies define themselves by their business model and sometimes fail to recognize the things that happen outside the sphere created by its linear narrative. The narrative can lead you astray in many different ways. You may, for instance, find emerging opportunities to be incompatible with your business model and ignore them – Lars decides to stick with selling adhesive tape for colostomy bags and ignores the potential new business. Another aspect to take into account is that stories outlined by business models don't behave in the way we are used to in the world of movie scripts and novels. The two most significant differences are that, in the world of business, there are a constant introduction of new characters and a constant change of conditions.

- **Constant introduction of new characters**
In the late 1990s, there were a number of incumbent search engines, including Lycos, Altavista and Yahoo. The next ten years, however, would be dominated by a complete unknown coming from out of nowhere – or from the heads of its two founders in Silicon Valley, to be more precise. Backrub was founded in 1998, but since the founders didn't much like the name, they switched to Whatbox. Feeling that it sounded too much like a porn site, they settled for a misspelled version of the number googol.[7] This story is replicated constantly. Industries are disrupted by unexpected competitors and new technologies. The innovative spirit of business makes

for an exciting investment climate but poor storytelling. Imagine "Little Red Riding Hood" with a new character introduced on every other page. Many companies still hold the narrative model dear, though, and plan their future in a linear, ordered sense. They make incremental budget increases only to be surprised by reality lurking around the next corner to make their plans obsolete.

● Constant change of conditions

In the early 1990s, US telecom giant AT&T produced a series of advertisements intended to thrill its customers with the promise of tomorrow's cutting-edge technology. The pay-off was "You Will", and the campaign featured all the usual sci-fi props like picture telephony and in-car navigation tools. One of the films featured a man lying in a deckchair on a beach grabbing a document from a mobile printer: "Have you ever sent a fax from the beach? You will!" What AT&T failed to take into account was the unpredictability of innovation. When we make predictions about future technologies, we have a hard time seeing beyond what today's machinery can do. A notorious miscalculation took place in New York in the late eighteenth century. People were warned that if they didn't change their way of living, travelling and consuming, there would be a three-metre layer of manure covering the entire island of Manhattan ("Look at all the horses we use today and imagine how many we will need if we continue to grow like we have done").[8] The reason innovation is such an elusive force is that people tend to assume things are impossible until they are made possible. That has been

People tend to assume things are impossible until they are made possible

the case with everything from supersonic flight to curing malaria. The future is not a fixed entity where the same rules apply as today.

We also tend to mispredict future customer demands. Entire industries are built around an assumption about customer behaviour, only to collapse when the fickle buyers start chasing the next big thing. It's rather poignant that the word for customer in Turkish is *müşteri* and is pronounced mystery.

These two transformative forces, new characters and new conditions, act in unison to continually derail companies in their quest for profits. Their origin, however, is one and the same: people's heads.

Serendipitous innovation

The haphazard, random way in which new ideas are formed stands in stark contrast to the ordered process of innovation that large firms have set up. You can even argue that these are two different approaches in conflict with each other. On one side is the tinkering individual with little or no resources. On the other side stands the collectivist climate of large corporations and government incentive programmes. Both sides are hoping for that rare moment of serendipity when the parts click into place and a new, promising idea emerges. Serendipity plays an uncomfortably large part in innovation. Think of Compeed™, or

> The origin of ideas is seldom plans and processes but rather mistakes, mispredictions and goalless experimentation

Per Gessle composing "The Look" by randomly pressing buttons. Think of Post-it notes, nylon, penicillin, Viagra and many other groundbreaking products. They were all results of fortunate accidents in the form of forgotten Petri dishes or failed heart medicines. The origin of ideas is seldom plans and processes but rather mistakes, mispredictions and goalless experimentation.

"The end of surprise would be the end of science", as the historian Robert Friedel wrote in the 2001 essay "Serendipity is no accident". Unfortunately, throughout history, many have tried to combat the uncontrollable nature of progress. From Church and clergy outlawing medical practioners to modern-day management literature, which attempts to describe every single business success story as an expected outcome of a series of carefully considered decisions. Henry Mintzberg, a business professor, takes the opposite view and argues that what we call strategy is really just "a pattern in a chaotic stream of action".[9] Similarly, successful economic clusters around the world – as with software in Silicon Valley or movies in Bollywood – are merely accidental, claims Nobel laureate economist Paul Krugman: "The specific location of a particular microindustry is to a large degree indeterminate, and history-dependent. But once a pattern of specialization is established, for whatever reason, that pattern gets 'locked in' by the cumulative gains from trade."[10]

One of the past century's most intense battle of ideas has been between creationists, who believe there is a maker who has made all living things according to some kind of master plan, and Darwinists, who argue that there is no such thing as a maker. Evolution is a meaningless process in that there is no ulterior motive or meaning. Species struggle to survive and adapt to new conditions. Some succeed over time while others fail. We can apply these two different perspectives to business and politics. In business, some people have a strong faith in the idea of a common, cohesive, long-term goal while others view economic activity as a random, disorganized stream of ideas and actions. In the world of politics, some believe in a strong state and vision that can shape countries and cities and point them in a certain direction – look at China or Dubai. Others take a laissez-faire approach and argue that nations and cities function at their best when nobody and everybody is in charge.

Whether by chance or planning, ideas can be defined as collisions. Between brains and problems, between different materials and technologies, and between different people. One of the most common definitions of creativity is as a combination of two familiar ideas into something new – think of a walkie-talkie mating with a telephone and having a mobile phone as offspring. "Creativity is connecting things," as Apple founder Steve Jobs once eloquently put it. Collisions tend to happen in areas that are densely populated, and cities are the prime example of this. An urban area is a combustible combination of different backgrounds, ethnicities, cultures, values and ideals. Urban economist Jane Jacobs says that "[even] work that we consider rural has originated in cities … it is directly built on city economies and city work".[11] Beyond geography, the World Wide Web is another accelerator of creativity, with people easily peering into the minds of

Ideas can be defined as collisions

complete strangers, glancing over the border at another country or taking a sneak peak behind the closed doors of companies and laboratories. The connectivity of the Internet and the increase in the world's population not only breed but boost innovation. It is in megacities like Tokyo, New York or Mumbai, melting pots of unpredictability, that we will witness the rise of many new trends, fads and ideas in the coming decades. There is no way to predict what creative marvels this will result in.

Companies are entities frozen in time

Now compare the vivid, experimental origin of ideas with the dull, orderly workplace that many of us spend our days in to earn a salary. What happened along the way?

My high-school physics teacher may have had the answer: in the very first class I attended with him, he took a big pile of papers and threw them on the floor. "Nature strives for disorder," he said. Without human hands to pile papers together and man-made structures to shelter them from the elements, paper would vanish in the wind or break apart from moisture.

This movement towards disorder can be seen wherever we look in nature. People, however, are ill equipped and unwilling to be at the mercy of Mother Nature. We invent routines, structures and meaning to protect us against becoming the paper pile. This is what happens as ideas solidify into a business and the one-man company grows into a multinational behemoth. Anyone who has worked for a start-up and its entrepreneurial founder knows what a struggle it can be. Decisions are made in an instant, poorly communicated and changed on a whim. It's like being thrown into the trunk of a car and taken for a joyride. Entrepreneurs make poor managers. If a company is to outlive its founder, it needs to bureaucratize. The thrilling sense of being a trailblazing pioneer is replaced by the gravity of running a serious business whose purpose is to serve customers while keeping its employees and owners happy.

This makes companies vulnerable in the face of the unexpected. With the rise of formalized structures comes a decline in the kind of creative improvisation that characterizes a start-up. This is something Ray Ozzie noticed when he came aboard as Chief Software Architect at Microsoft. Replacing founder Bill Gates, Ozzie realized that Microsoft was an excellent company. Well run, great products, high margins, well-managed product development cycles and so on. But it was all a bit too well run, and that's when Ozzie formulated his vision: "Microsoft [has] to think and operate more like a start-up."[12] A risk-management executive that I interviewed at a large telecommunications firm described a similar culture clash in her company: "My profession is all about trying to discover risks before they become a liability for the company. It's a job of constantly asking 'what if?' … In this company, people aren't used to that kind of imaginative approach so they just throw large piles of money at problems to make them go away."

To understand what happens in the transition between the nimble, entrepreneurial start-up and its older, wiser, less creative older brother, it's useful to look at what happens when people decide to start exercising more. A gym instructor I met in London described it by drawing a curve with a steep, vertical beginning that then levels off into a flat line: "People who start exercise programmes make huge gains in the first few weeks as they regain lost stamina, shed excess pounds and add a bit muscle tissue to arms and legs. Then something happens. The body doesn't respond as much to the exercise and we, in turn, settle into a habitual routine with treadmills and weights. We enter a 'comfort plateau'." This plateau is also what mature companies face, but economists like to refer to it as "declining marginal rate of return". Management guru Peter Drucker explains that "it is difficult for management to accept unexpected [turns of events, because] all of us tend to believe that anything that has lasted a fair amount of time must be 'normal' and go on 'forever.'"[13]

Professor Don Sull at the London Business School has taken this idea of solidified companies a step farther and coined the phrase "active inertia" to describe why certain companies fail to adapt to changing conditions and perish. "Active inertia is the condition of doing what you've always done – and doing it well – but missing the curve in the road. It's not what you do that gets you in trouble; it's when you keep doing what you've always done."[14]

I noticed this when I consulted for a Scandinavian cinema chain. Cinema visits have been flat in the past decade, so cinemas and movie distributors alike need to come up with new, creative ways in which to attract more punters. We started discussing exciting new ways in which to lure people to the movies. Being a father of small children, I found that my ideas tended to revolve around things like "Saturday morning pyjama cinema for kids" or making a ninety-minute express edit featuring the most critically acclaimed movies of the past two years, since fatherhood has kept me away from the cinema for some time. To my surprise, the energy in the room was running lower by the minute, with most of the senior executives either shrugging or coughing when I shared my ideas. Then the VP of business development cleared his throat and said the following: "Magnus, before we start discussing new ideas, you need to understand that our industry is *special*. It's *not* like other industries. It's full of rules and regulation and our customers tend to be conservative."

[handwritten margin note: Industry Patriotism]

I am not berating this company for rejecting ideas that might not have been particularly good to begin with. What I found striking was that the four words "our industry is special" were spoken with such pride, and that people around the room were nodding vigorously in agreement. We can call this "industry patriotism", since it resembles the blinding, nationalist self-love that can lead both politicians and football fans astray as they fail to correctly assess national accounts or World Cup odds respectively.

A system immune to new ideas

We can think of corporate resistance to change as an immune system and describe it as follows:[15]

$$r = f(n^m)$$
where
r = internal resistance to new ideas
and is a function of

n = number of employees

rising exponentially with

m = number of management levels

The human beings that make up *n* and *m* can be divided into three groups based on their relationship to new opportunities and unexpected situations: *change lovers, change haters* and *change reluctants*. I saw all three groups in action at a recent conference where Pilates balls were used to seat people instead of chairs. Some people came into the room and could not wait to get on a ball and start bouncing. These were the change lovers who thrive when facing the unexpected. No matter what new ideas they are facing, their response will always be an enthusiastic "yes, let's go!" A second group of people came into the room and stared at the balls with incomprehension, even anger. These were the change haters. They ran across the room and sat down on the one row of chairs available at the back. No matter how good the new idea is, change haters will never accommodate it.

The absolute majority at this event, however, can be characterized as change reluctants. They came into the room, folded their arms and waited. They seemed intrigued by the idea of sitting on a Pilates ball but did not want to be the first to sit down on one. So they lingered. When a critical mass of change lovers had taken their seats, however, the change reluctants couldn't wait to get on a ball and join them, but they had needed that first group of people to show the way. This pattern repeats itself in companies and markets on a daily basis. A handful of players exploit shifts and unexpected opportunities early only to be followed by the reluctant majority, with some change haters firmly parked on the sidelines declaring their mistrust.

Useful interruptions

Hoping for change-loving colleagues and customers to make us brave is a slow yet effective way to shake things up in companies that have stagnated on the comfort plateau. There are others.

The Baltimore and Ohio Railroad Museum was built to honour one of the oldest railroad tracks in the United States and has "one of the most significant collections of railroad treasures in the world and ... the largest collection of 19th century locomotives in the US".[16] In February 2003, after a heavy snowstorm, the entire roof of the museum collapsed and destroyed large parts of the collection. An event like this can demoralize staff and damage reputations significantly. At this museum the opposite happened. "Dealing with the collapse made the staff more nimble," explained the *Harvard Business Review*. "The organization adeptly handled the setback, raising funds and plunging into fresh challenges such as hosting large-scale events, expanding educational programs, and establishing a train-restoration facility ... A disruption, whether positive or negative, may create a blank sheet on which the organization can reinvent itself."[17]

I had a similar experience of organizational disruptions while working on an assignment with a world-famous architect in the early 2000s. The project was to construct the head office for a large, financial conglomerate. One of the last areas to be designed was the reception area, and the architect asked me for good ideas about how to make a positive first impression on visitors by doing something special. I remembered reading somewhere that Nike, the sports clothing brand, had a small river running through its lobby. The idea was that people would have to jump over the river and thus "earn" their place at the reception desk – a suitable concept for a company that takes pride in helping everyone perform better. When I told the architect about this idea, his eyes lit up. "Of course, what a brilliant concept! Let's do it!"

A year later, the office opened complete with a river running through reception. There was just one small problem. The architect had used some creative licence when interpreting the idea of a river and it now looked more like a swimming pool embedded in the floor than the lively creek I had envisioned. Furthermore, it was constructed in the same material as the floor itself, so it became nearly invisible. During the first few days after the opening, more than a dozen people either stepped or fell into the "river". The reception staff even had to keep a stock of dry socks behind the counter for unfortunate guests. The client decided to put a glass floor over it and turn it into a Japanese garden instead.

> Interruptions, inconveniences and unexpected events can be effective in changing the fortunes of a company

The idea that I have never been able to shake off completely, however, is that making customers of a financial firm accidentally fall into a pool of cold water might have prevented the financial meltdown of 2008. How so? Just like unexpected events sharpening our senses and roof collapses "waking up" staff, unexpectedly falling into water when entering an office could have shaken up the minds of bankers and brokers and made them think twice about what it was they were buying and selling. This is mere speculation of course, but based on the knowledge that interruptions, inconveniences and unexpected events can be effective in changing the fortunes of a company or an industry for the better.

Conflict and insecurity as leadership tools

Something that has proved surprisingly effective in generating positive outcomes is conflict. Although it is something many try to avoid, debates and confrontation can be healthy and stir things up considerably in companies that have grown stale.

Take the ill-fated Lehman Brothers as a warning example. It was described by *Fortune* magazine as "one of Wall Street's most harmonious firms".[18] Dick Fuld, the company's notorious CEO, had expended significant effort on transforming the company from a place that "was all about the 'me'. My job. My people. Pay me ... [It] was a great example of how *not* to do it",[19] as Fuld described it. Again, we can only speculate as to whether a less "harmonious" Lehman Brothers, where people questioned and challenged each other, would have met the same fate as the

> It is hard for a large company to deliver groundbreaking, transformative new ideas

one that sank an entire industry in September 2008, but it's self-evident that a certain level of disagreement inside a firm is healthy. Take creativity, for instance. For the past decade, it has been one of the biggest buzzwords in the corporate world, and executives have been put through numerous creativity seminars and fed catchphrases like "think outside the box" or "challenge our assumptions". The effectiveness of this restrained type of creativity is unclear. It is unlikely to foster the kind of personal tinkering Lars engaged in to create Compeed™ or the kind of creative destruction that more disruptive innovations tend to display.

It is, in other words, hard for a large company that takes pride in its teamwork and processes to deliver groundbreaking, transformative new ideas. The large firm is often reluctant to place emphasis solely on the individual, and it also requires too much certainty in order to accurately budget for the next fiscal year. Certainty is the enemy of innovation. Just think of nation-states. Nordic economies are often placed atop indices of creativity and innovation. A study by the Boston Consulting Group, for example, rates Iceland, Finland, Denmark and Sweden as being in the top eleven most innovative countries in the world.[20] Four of the five Nordic countries. But not Norway. Furthermore, neither Russia nor Saudi Arabia is on that list. What these three diverse countries share is an abundance of natural resources, primarily oil and gas. Economists refer to this as "the resource curse" to describe what happens when states discover oil or gas. Instead of mining

Certainty is the enemy of innovation

Certainty curse
oil + gas

people's heads for new ideas, they drill more holes in the ground, and innovation stagnates.

"Medici effect"

In this book, we can refer to it as "the certainty curse", where the promise of guaranteed growth kills the catalysing thrill of the unknown needed to spark innovation. Adds the innovation blog The Medici Effect: "Knowing that a certain income level can be sustained for a long period of time may be nice and cushy, but it doesn't promote the risk-taking that is needed to start new businesses and innovate."[21]

It is unwise to place safety first in innovation, claims Wikipedia founder Jimmy Wales. If you want to create something radical, you cannot and should not be held back by alarmist "what ifs?" and constrictive "what mights?" He uses a restaurant metaphor to illustrate: "Imagine that your new dining establishment intends to sell steaks, so therefore you'll need to provide sharp knives to your customers. Knives are also weapons and people could stab one another with them, so rather than booths and tables, you'd better lock your customers in individual cells to prevent that behaviour."[22]

🌀 A climate for change

In 2003, the then US defence secretary Donald Rumsfeld won the "Foot in Mouth" prize awarded by the British Plain English Campaign for "the most nonsensical remark made by a public figure". The ill-famed phrase for which he earned the award was as follows: "There are known knowns; there are things we know we know. We also know there are known unknowns; that is to say we know there are some things we do not know. But there are also unknown unknowns – the ones we don't know we don't know."[23] Rumsfeld's statement is certainly no marvel of elo-

---

How do you prepare yourself and your organization for something you can't even imagine?

---

quence, but among the tangled spaghetti of words, he is pointing out something interesting. "Unknown unknowns" is the vital ingredient in what we perceive to be unexpected.

Rumsfeld

There are things we can imagine, but these will never surprise us in the way the things that lie beyond our imagination will. Steven Barnett, a futurist who helped Steven Spielberg design the set pieces in *Minority Report*, puts it as follows: "The future isn't just an extension of the past. It can be something brand new. Something we have never seen before."[24] So how do you prepare yourself and your organization for something you can't even imagine? The answer is that you build a culture adapted to uncertainty. "Whatever causes the next crisis, it will be different, so you need something that can deal with the unexpected. That's culture,"[25] as one banker put it in the aftermath of the financial crisis. Here are some ingredients needed for a culture suited to deal with the unexpected:

Made to move

Why are some firms quicker to respond when the unexpected strikes? This was a question posed by a Harvard case study[26] written in the aftermath of the 2004 Indian Ocean tsunami. The disaster had left many dead, injured and in dire need of help. Governments were slow to react, but news organizations and travel companies were not. In fact, when the Swedish state eventually got around to

Dominant Response Theory – Problem solving

Travel Companies

helping its citizens abroad, travel companies had already been assisting victims for days.

What was the difference between the sluggish governments and the responsive travel companies? The answer is something called dominant response. Dominant response theory argues that every organization has an instinctive way of responding whenever something happens. News organizations, for example, are quick to mobilize and start reporting whenever the unexpected strikes. The dominant response of travel companies is solving problems quickly. Guests complaining about noise in the middle of the night? Solve the problem. No hotel room available although the guest has had a confirmatory e-mail? Solve the problem.

When the tsunami struck, it was no coincidence that media teams and travel companies were quick to respond while governments – whose dominant response is to discuss things, analyse and make politically loaded statements – were left far behind. Companies that want to thrive in a world of unexpected threats and opportunities need to make swift action part of their dominant response. To quote the admired US low-fare airline Southwest: "We have a strategy – it's called doing things."

Succeeding by failing

The Nespresso coffee machine by Nestlé has become ubiquitous in modern kitchens and hotel lobbies around the world. Its road to success was hardly straight.

"Nestlé started working on the technology in 1970 and filed its first patent in 1976. It was another decade before it was ready to start selling Nespresso pods and machines. Thereafter the business lost money for a decade. But now it is one of Nestlé's fastest-growing products. Sales have been increasing by 30% a year and reached nearly SFr3 billion in 2009."[27] It is, in other words, a success story forty years in the making. That kind of longevity and patience is rare in today's speed-oriented business world. It may, however, be necessary. In a world full of rocky roads and surprises, we will doubtless miss many short-term trends and fads, but we can craft a long-term vision and allow ourselves to fail a few times before we succeed.

Nespresso was not the result of stellar forecasting in the early 1970s, but of patient owners. Furthermore, we can assume that many other patents were registered along with Nespresso in the early 1970s but failed to reach fruition along the way. Businesses have for a long time talked about the many merits of focus, but what if business success is the result of doing many different things and allowing most of them to fail?

We can call this way of innovating "Darwinnovation", because the perspective Charles Darwin added to biology was that evolution was the result of diversity. Many different species compete for survival and only some will adapt perfectly to their surroundings and pass their genes on to their offspring. Similarly, companies like Nestlé file hundreds of patents and watch most of them fail. The best way of anticipating an uncertain future is to have many different ideas of what it will look like and make *microbets*. A microbet is an idea or invention with a minimum amount of resources invested,

> The best way of anticipating an uncertain future is to have many different ideas of what it will look like

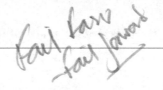

so if and when it fails, the losses will be limited. That is the magic of Silicon Valley's famous proverb "Fail Fast Forward".[28] We should take risks. We should fail. But when we do, let's do it quickly and learn something from it in the process.

The clueless leader

"If you want to be innovative, don't hire thirty-five-year olds!"[29] These are the words of gaming company Electronic Arts founder Bing Gordon. What he means is that the thirtysomething employee is unlikely to take risks because of his or her large mortgage-and-young-children combo. Risk-taking and the innovative ideas it spawns are to be found in maverick teenagers or people in the fearless fifties. How about leadership? In uncertain, surprise-laden times, who is better suited to not just manage a company but also help it excel? Chasing the perfect leader has been a favourite sport of management writers and academic research for years, so without trying to add yet another utopian personality profile to the mix, let us challenge the very idea of a leader. Why do we need a person to lead us and show us the way? What if the ultimate corporate facilitator is a person who does not attempt to lead and makes no claims about seeing the road ahead?

I have met such a person. He is the founder and chairman of a successful real estate company in the UK. Founded in the late 1970s, the company has been growing in double-digit increments in most fiscal years since. When I asked him what his secret was and where he planned to take his company next, he looked at me, seemingly puzzled: "Whenever people ask me that in boardrooms or at conferences, I just shrug," he said, "and say that I have no bloody idea." It sounded like a smug statement from someone who has found long-term success a little too easily, so I checked with some of the managers in the company. They had the same attitude. The less they knew about the future, the better. "We call it 'management by staying out of the way,'" as one of them joked.

Think of the path most people's careers take. It's often more of a crooked line than a straight corporate ladder. Success does require hard work and good ideas, but these are rarely enough. What defines the careers of hard-working, smart people who find success tends to be chance meetings and happy accidents.

Before I found my passion as a trendspotter, I was lost in the world of management consulting and advertising for nearly a decade. I'm not an exception. The question "What should I be?" remains unanswered to a certain extent for all of us throughout life nowadays. With the emergence of a middle-class workforce who want and need their job to be more than a source of income, we have merely seen the beginning of the meaning-seeking worker. It will be tempting for many managers and executives to become the provider of meaning and context for these workers, but that would require them to sell a strong vision of and a clear path to the future, which can ultimately be not only deceptive but constrictive. The clueless leader makes for a more frustrating character, but his or her chorus of constant "I don't knows" will ensure that more ideas are released into the world unobstructed by their own concept of what lies ahead.

👄 In need of the unexpected

The disorganized origin of new innovations and the unexpected turns of markets mean that the idea of a company as a fixed, rigid entity is beginning to look somewhat outdated. This chapter has pointed out some examples of what its replacement could look like. It's not a question of finding one replacement but rather of finding many different, often contradictory, new ways of getting things done.

> The idea of a company as a fixed, rigid entity is beginning to look somewhat outdated

This is why the current focus on entrepreneurship by governments and schools is fortunate. The entrepreneur is guided by his or her own ideas of how to do things. If what we are seeing is a long-term societal shift to a world where starting up your own company becomes the norm, we will witness a veritable explosion of new ideas.

Meanwhile, multinationals will not perish overnight, as their critics often claim. The demise of businesses has indeed been exaggerated for dramatic effect. With the exception of some well-publicized corporate fiascos, most companies don't just vanish into thin air, but fade away slowly over many years. A combination of complacency and a loss of that innovative, chaotic flair that younger companies often display slowly leads these older giants on to a path to oblivion. A path that can be paved with some terrific business opportunities, but whose destination is ultimately destructive.

The constant threat and promise of the unexpected keep companies on their feet. Similarly, a company that has only had to swim in shallow and calm waters will capsize as soon as a tidal wave hits – as an example of this, think about what has happened to newspapers in the past decade, which have moved from cosy geographic monopolies into a world of online free-for-alls. The next chapter will look at what happens when these tidal waves hit not just companies and industries but entire societies.

Chapter 3 – The Game

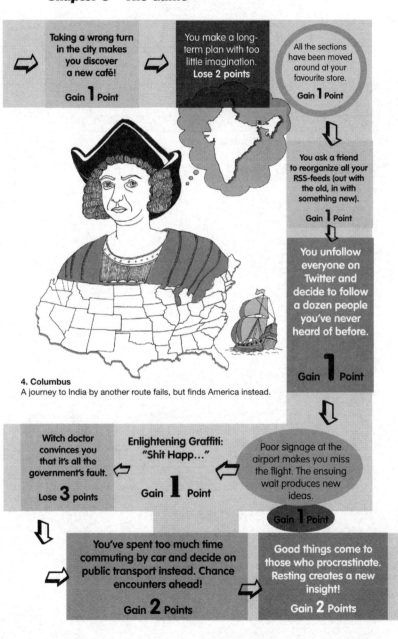

Taking a wrong turn in the city makes you discover a new café!

Gain **1** Point

You make a long-term plan with too little imagination.
Lose 2 points

All the sections have been moved around at your favourite store.

Gain **1** Point

You ask a friend to reorganize all your RSS-feeds (out with the old, in with something new).

Gain **1** Point

You unfollow everyone on Twitter and decide to follow a dozen people you've never heard of before.

Gain **1** Point

4. Columbus
A journey to India by another route fails, but finds America instead.

Witch doctor convinces you that it's all the government's fault.

Lose **3** points

Enlightening Graffiti: "Shit Happ…"

Gain **1** Point

Poor signage at the airport makes you miss the flight. The ensuing wait produces new ideas.

Gain **1** Point

You've spent too much time commuting by car and decide on public transport instead. Chance encounters ahead!

Gain **2** Points

Good things come to those who procrastinate. Resting creates a new insight!

Gain **2** Points

4 Hurricane winds of change

How societies collide with the unexpected

> "A thing long expected takes the form of the unexpected when at last it comes"
>
> Mark Twain

What should I be?

A popular board game in the 1960s was called "What Should I Be?" It focused on inspiring young boys and girls about what kind of profession they wanted to pursue. Boys, the game said, were ideal as doctors, astronauts and scientists, while girls were poised to become nurses, air hostesses and ballet dancers. The game also contained a series of cards which awarded the player a set of skills or personality traits. Boys could become intelligent, a quality that would set them on a straight path to a Nobel Prize, and girls could start suffering from clumsiness or sloppy make-up, something that would eternally disqualify them from serving drinks at 30,000 feet for a living.

"What Should I Be?" and innumerable old TV series reveal how societies change in many different dimensions. It is not just a matter of some new technologies disappearing and new professions cropping up. Values change. Behaviour changes. People change. Societies fragment and fuse. Some modernize and progress while others collapse completely. The central theme of this chaotic, multivariate change is the unexpected, whose magic wand constantly transforms societies and sends them on a path into an unknown future.

In 1993, my friend Nicklas and I were engaged in a "What Should I Be?" of sorts. As we threw ideas around between us as to what we wanted to do with our lives, at least for the next few years, I was torn between my head – urging me to go to business school – and my heart, which was firmly set on becoming a film-maker. Nicklas, on the other hand, had this whimsical idea of wanting to study Chinese. My response was something akin to "what a waste of time!" Two decades later, Nicklas can look back on – and indeed forward to – a prosperous career, due in no small part to his Chinese-speaking skills. The question one – or at least I – must ask is why the idea of studying Chinese in the early 1990s seemed like such a far-fetched choice when China was to become one of the economic superpowers of the world. The answer reveals itself when we study *how* China grew from the early 1990s and into the coming decades.

◖◗ The Ketchup Effect

What is interesting in Figure 1 is the shape of the curve. Instead of climbing in a slow, predictable manner, it seemingly explodes in the early 2000s as the wealth of China skyrockets. This would explain why few of us took China seriously in the 1990s. I remember reading a book called *China Rising* while at business school in the mid-1990s and thinking that what it described was some far-off future scenario where there would be household robots and cure-all pills. Growth curves like China's trick us into

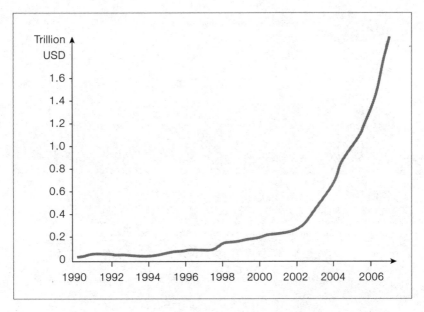

Fig 1 ● China's foreign currency reserve in trillion USD, 1990–2008

Source: IMF

thinking nothing much is happening until everything seems to happen all at once. The growth of the two best-known social media brands of the past few years displays a similar curve – see Figures 2 and 3.

If you had organized a conference on the subjects of China and social media in the mid-1990s, the turnout would have been a handful of people with either extreme foresight or a lot of time to waste. In the second decade of this century, these are by far the most common topics in conferences and on business bestseller lists. This exponential curve – a flat beginning followed by a near-vertical

> A development can look linear and predictable at first, only to explode overnight

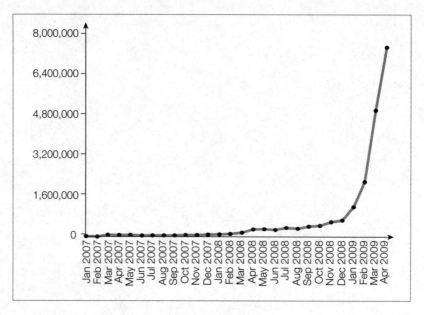

Fig 2 ● New Twitter users by month, 2007–09

Source: RJ Metrics

explosion – is sometimes referred to as the Ketchup
Effect. It's a suitable name. When pouring ketchup from
the iconic Heinz glass bottle, you get absolutely nothing
at first, then a small drop of reddish liquid that you want
to avoid having on your food, then a large gob of ketchup
potentially drowning everything on the plate. Nothing,
then a little bit, then everything – the Ketchup Effect.

What makes this curve so deceptive is that you never
really know what it is you are looking at. A development
can look linear and predictable at first, only to explode
overnight. Take the financial collapse of 2008 as an
example of this. When banks reported losses due to sub-
prime loans in the summer of 2007, the common opinion
was that this problem would be contained and handled

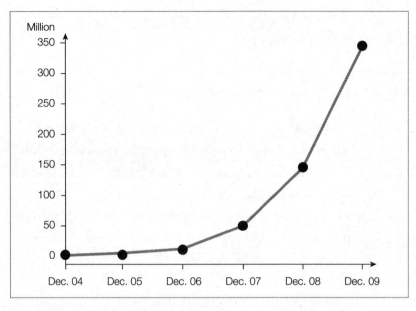

Fig 3 ● Number of active Facebook users, 2004–09

Source: Fast Company

effortlessly by the banks themselves. Only a year later, the system imploded, burdened by an intricate web of obscure derivatives, swaps and mountains of debt. Nothing, then a little bit, and then everything.

The Ketchup Effect is unpredictable not because trivial things suddenly become world-changing, but because most things stay small and insignificant, only for a handful of them to become supernovas. The miraculous growth of China, the rise of Facebook, Twitter or the iPhone, American sub-prime loans dictating the direction of the world economy, Icelandic volcanic ash shutting down Europe's entire airspace – all unfathomable until they became household phenomena and subjects for dinner-table conversations. The question is why the

Ketchup Effect occurs and why it seems to strike so often in the 21st century.

The change of change

Globalization is complicated, and in the past decade writers have gone to considerable lengths to find suitable metaphors to simplify it. Some argue that globalization is like a sand pile, others that it is making the world flat again, the way it was perceived to be before Magellan's travels proved otherwise. It has been likened to an electronic herd, to a worldwide spider's web and to a global village.

Regardless of the metaphor, the conclusions are similar: globalization makes the world interconnected and unpredictable. Small things can have a big impact and the pace of change quickens. Where financial transactions or political statements were once geographically confined, they can now alter the world's fortunes in milliseconds. Globalization creates stability on one hand, with security and national interests increasingly intertwined across borders, but it also creates a world where change happens quickly and in unpredictable ways.

> Globalization makes the world interconnected and unpredictable

Small things — big impact [handwritten annotation]

In sharp contrast to the combustible nature of globalization's network effects stands the human brain. It is unlikely that we will see a sudden surge in the numbers of people being able to play a symphony by Brahms on the violin or making Nobel Prize-winning scientific discoveries. The reason is that human learning is slow and gradual, and requires years of practice, whereas e-mail spam, financial transactions or Twitter membership require only the click of a few buttons.

The basic hazards of linear thinking

At least once every generation the point is made that we live in a messy world where things move ever faster, so one might simply sigh and add "so what?" That would be to miss an important lesson, however, since human beings are creatures capable of foresight. When our ability to plan ahead collides with a change of pace in societal development, we risk taking wrong turns and being led astray.

One example of that is the way computer studies were taught in schools in the early 1980s. The school that I went to had purchased a series of brand-new, expensive personal computers. We had to share a machine in groups of four. The curriculum consisted mainly of lessons in which we were taught about the insides of the computer and BASIC programming. BASIC is a programming language that enabled the more digitally gifted of the class to make the computer write the word "Hello!" on the screen an infinite number of times. For those of us who are prone to making mistakes when typing, BASIC programming was sheer misery, the words "syntax error" appearing endlessly and the teacher having to correct our typographical mishaps. This authoritarian way of teaching rested on the correct assumption that

> What is impossible today might be a mundane everyday task tomorrow

personal computers were here to stay, but it also assumed that BASIC programming would be a useful future skill, much like using a typewriter had been a generation earlier. Today, we can see the humour in this as virtually nobody programmes BASIC on their laptops or handheld devices. We download movies, write e-mails, have video-conferences and look at images of family members or recent adventures – all for the price of what half a keyboard cost in the early 1980s.

The reason for the ill-conceived curriculums of the past is the Ketchup Effect of Moore's Law. Simply explained, Moore's Law states that computing power will increase exponentially while its cost decreases equally fast. The exponential curve makes long-term planning of the kind needed in education very hard. What is impossible today might be a mundane everyday task tomorrow. This is a common feature of technological development. The economist Paul Romer, for example, has measured the improvement in the standard of living over time, with the amount of light you could buy for every extra hour worked being the metric used to describe standard of living. If this metric strikes you as odd, it is because the question of light has been made completely redundant in the past century since the invention of the light bulb. As Figure 4 shows, however, the search for light was for many thousands of years one of the most pressing issues for mankind. Then candles, oil lamps and gasoline came along, enabling us to buy increasing quantities of light for our hard-earned wages, but when electricity started to illuminate society, light became almost too cheap to meter and nobody in a reasonably developed country

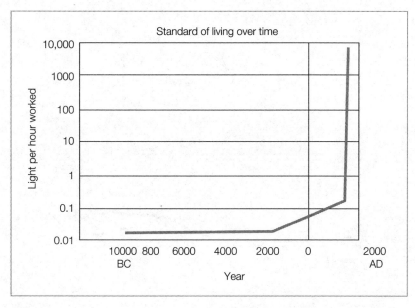

Fig 4 ● Affordable light per hour worked (average), 10.000 BC–AD 2010
Source: Paul Romer

has to stay at work late on Tuesday evenings to afford it.

Energy use in Sweden is another example of technology taking sharp turns. In Figure 5 on page 100, you can see the various sources of energy used in Sweden from 1800 onwards. What is striking is the drastic developments of the 1970s that transformed smooth predictable curves into a scribble of lines intertwining. The OPEC oil crisis of October 1973 made Sweden switch to nuclear power almost overnight. Today, predicting future energy sources has become very difficult, since the combination of expensive oil and the battle against carbon dioxide emissions has created a free-for-all where innovative start-ups and scientific breakthroughs compete with energy-industry

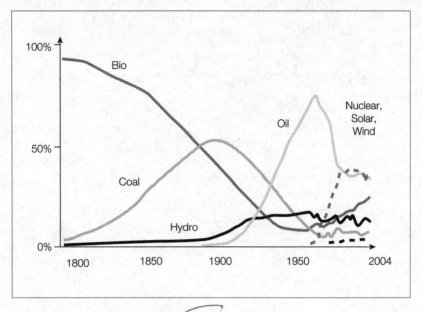

Fig 5 ● Sweden's energy use by type, 1800–2006

Source: Power Circle, 2009

incumbents to win the hearts, minds and wallets of future customers. Where we once had to choose between biofuel, coal, oil or nuclear power, there is now a plethora of exotic new alternatives ranging from wind and solar power to energy generated by algae or genetically modified bacteria.

Charles Darwin once claimed that evolution is blind to the future, and these examples serve to illustrate that people too are future-blind. When developments in the real world outpace our minds, we can only hope to enjoy the ride into an unknown future. Says futurist Ray Kurzweil, who has expended considerable effort on showing how the future is often driven by exponential – not linear – development: "[What if we asked] cavemen and women: 'Well, gee, what would you like to have?'

And they'd say, 'Well, we'd like a bigger rock to keep the animals out of our cave and we'd like to keep this fire from burning out.' And you'd say, 'Well, don't you want a good website? What about your Second Life habitat?' They couldn't imagine these things. And those are just the technological innovations."[1]

Darwin's dangerous idea

The examples used so far have something more in common than just unpredictability; they are also man-made. Technological innovation doesn't just happen. It is the result of visionary people putting considerable effort into making and marketing a new idea. Science writer Matt Ridley argues that man is the only species capable of innovation. Whereas other creatures use tools, these don't change between generations the way man-made technologies do. The question is why. Ridley argues that the reason is man's collective brain, the combined thinking power and the resulting ideas created by human beings in large groups, and refers to it as "ideas having sex".[2] This is a way of looking at progress. Not just as a single breakthrough invention, but as a collective effort to generate new ideas and try new things.

This, in turn, creates a self-organizing system that no one individual controls. Emergence, as it's sometimes called, makes societal development behave erratically. Take cities, for example. As the world has urbanized in the past century, new kinds of living and working have followed suit. Take single households: a rarity in the first half of the twentieth century is now becoming the norm in more and more cities around the world, reaching a whopping 61 per cent in my home town of Stockholm, Sweden. Or consider Gay Pride parades. Where homosexuality was once frowned upon, even to the extent of being considered a crime, a Pride parade is now a required feature for any city that wishes to convey an image of economic progress, innovative thinking and humane ideals.

I would argue that both single households and increased tolerance of homosexuality are direct consequences of more people living in cities, for what is a city if not a melting pot of different backgrounds, cultures and ideas? That is why I saw Gothic Lolita teenagers in Tokyo or Christian atheists demonstrating in London – they are mergers between two very different cultures that were once considered opposites.

There is, however, another way of creating a city nowadays. Emergent behaviour tends to flourish in a city that has been growing slowly but surely over decades, giving a common sense of identity time to mature ("I am a Stockholmer" or "I am a New Yorker", for example). What we have seen in the past decade, however, are "flash cities" that have quickly sprung up from the ground or grown disproportionately large very quickly. Take a city like Dubai, for example. While it has the same shiny skyscrapers and sprawling suburbs as any other modern city, it lacks a sense of collective identity and cohesion. The reason is that it did not develop in the bottom-up manner of London or Tokyo but was designed top-down and built quickly by the rulers of the emirate.

These two ways to create a city – top-down or bottom-up – can be likened to the ideas of creationism and

Darwinism. In the former, there is an intelligent designer who made Earth, nature and all its inhabitants. In the latter, all living things are merely the result of natural selection wherein species slowly adapt and evolve over time. This has been referred to as Darwin's dangerous idea. How can there not be an enlightened maker of all living things that display such beauty and complexity? If there is no maker, what happens to meaning and destiny? Can life really just be a random transfer of genes between generations? The answer is that emergent, self-governing systems have a remarkable capacity to display a kind of order in chaos. Take the World Wide Web as an example of this. It is neither governed nor structured by any one body, but is the result of millions of people collaborating and communicating.

Seeking shelter from the storm

In 1980, economist Julian Simon made a famous bet with biologist Paul Ehrlich. With resource prices having risen for the past decade, Ehrlich was convinced that what we were witnessing was resource depletion and that prices would continue to soar in the 1980s. Simon, on the other hand, argued that humanity would never run out of anything and challenged Ehrlich to choose any five resources whose prices he thought would increase and he, Simon, would bet against him. Choosing copper, chromium, nickel, tin and tungsten, Ehrlich accepted the bet and the race was on. A decade later, it was clear that pessimist Ehrlich had lost. All resources had dropped in price and continued to do so for another decade. (See Figure 6 on the following page.)

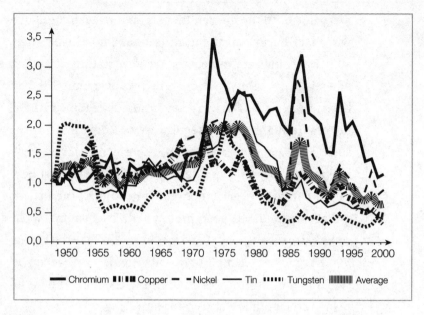

Fig 6 ● US commodity prices (inflation-adjusted), 1950–2010

Source: Wikipedia

Around the world, did people rejoice and thank Julian Simon for making a brave optimistic prediction at a time when things looked bad? No. Whereas Paul Ehrlich has been bestowed with a Macarthur Foundation Genius Award in 1990 for having promoted "greater public understanding of environmental problems", Simon has been more or less ignored by the public: "[He] always found it somewhat peculiar that neither his public wager with Ehrlich nor anything else that he did, said, or wrote seemed to make much of a dent on the world at large. For some reason he could never comprehend, people were inclined to believe the very worst about anything and everything; they were immune to contrary evidence just as if they'd been medically vaccinated against the force of fact."[3]

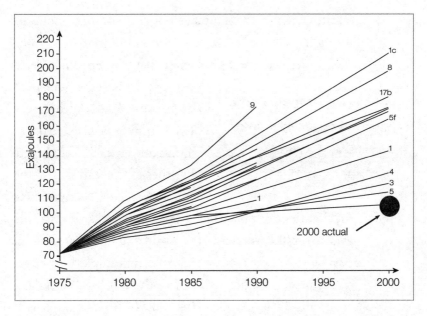

Fig 7 ● Projections of total US primary energy use, 1970 onwards
Source: Long Now Foundation

Why was the bet's loser rewarded while its winner was ignored? The reason is that thinking in negative scenarios is a kind of societal immune system, even if these scenarios never come true. Take energy use as an example of this. Making up scary scenarios about a future drained of energy forces us to adjust and invent new technologies. Look at Figure 7. It shows predictions of future primary energy use in the USA made in the 1970s. None of the predictions was able to match the actual energy use, not because they were too low but because they were too high.

From a young age we are told fairy tales and fables

> Thinking in negative scenarios is a kind of societal immune system

warning us about complacency and the false comfort brought on by an "all will work itself out in the end" attitude. One way we seek shelter in turbulent times is to explore worst-case scenarios to put the present in perspective. Another noticeable behaviour, however, is the complete antithesis. We can call it the "Ostrich Theory" because, like the flightless bird planting its head in the soil, we also hide away from the worries of the world and bury ourselves in past glories. Take comfort food as an example. One effect of the recent financial crisis was the return of nostalgia, especially in food and drink. Sales of beer and sweets shot up. Junk food treats of the 1970s came back with a vengeance, exemplified by the successful relaunch in the UK of the Arctic Roll – a frozen sponge cake said to taste "like cold cardboard". Think about the mind's reaction to the unexpected, described in an earlier chapter. When we stumble upon something strange and different, we retreat to familiar ground.

> When we stumble upon something strange and different, we retreat to familiar ground

This is how society reacted after the economic downturn, with nationalism replacing globalization and comfort foods replacing the culinary experimentation seen in the mid-2000s. At the height of the crisis, the USA even elected a leader who was often likened to either JFK or Lincoln. Barack Obama may have used the message "Change" to drive his campaign, but what he really represented for many Americans was a return to a time before all the trouble that George W. Bush had brought about – to a time when "our nation was still great". Historical metaphor is a frequently used tool to plant something new and different in the soil of familiarity. "This band is the new Beatles" or "This company is the next Microsoft." Metaphors like these see time not as a linear narrative or an exponential Ketchup Effect but as a slowly revolving cycle.

These thinking patterns – worst-case scenarios, nostalgia and historical metaphor – may help us cope better in times of difficulty, but they don't tell us how to act and what to do specifically. It might be more useful, then, to look at two of the most important components in life: your money and your job.

◐ Turbulence survival kit

As the world slid into recession in 2008 onwards, disposable income sank and people's spirits along with it. All around the world, depression statistics shot up, and with them indulgence in the many vices that accompany nervousness and unhealthy lifestyles, such as smoking and drinking. American psychologist Dan Gilbert argued that the cause, however, was not less money in itself but the decreased sense of certainty that went along with it: "An uncertain future leaves us stranded in an unhappy present with nothing to do but wait."[4]

Money is more than just a carrier of value; it is frozen freedom

What Gilbert hints at is the link between money and certainty. This link is not merely the perceived safety and comfort that comes along with a steady job and a fixed income; the link is money itself and what it represents. Money is more than just a carrier of value; it is frozen freedom. Think about it. What we envy in people richer than ourselves is the perceived freedom that they enjoy. If we save money, it is often to use at some point in the future, probably for something that we haven't really got a clear idea about just yet. Savings act as a cushion, protecting us against a hard collision with an unknown future. The simple remedy for people worried about uncertainty is to save more money.

> Work and money matter so much to people because they are refuges in an uncertain world

The second part of the survival toolkit is work itself. To quote philosopher Alain de Botton: "We are all five questions away from madness."[5] That is to say that life contains many riddles, especially concerning the meaning of it all. Questions about life's purpose and mortality lie at the deep end of existentialism, whose dark waters we may not wish to enter too often. Fortunately we can indulge in the trivialities of everyday office life, such as complaining about the copier or gossiping about the new manager. Everyday work provides millions of people with meaning by structuring the many chaotic and random events called life into neat portions of meetings and commutes. Work and money matter so much to people because they are refuges in an uncertain world.

◐ The upside of turbulence

When media channels cover unexpected events, they revel in stories about death and disaster, which put the unexpected in an unfavourable light. We have seen so far that unexpected events can have beneficial effects on brain and bottom line alike. What we haven't seen so far, however, is how the unexpected can have a positive effect on entire communities and countries. One of the most striking effects that negative events can have on a community is to create resilience. Like the human body developing antibodies after encountering a previously unfamiliar virus, cities and countries can generate a new sense of cohesion and durability by withstanding hardship and turbulence.

I have come across this a number of times in the past few years. After the near-bankruptcy of Greece, I visited Athens in the same week that newspapers around the world were filled with images of riots and protesters running amok. Having thought of cancelling my trip out of fear for my safety, I eventually decided to go nevertheless, but was prepared to step into a war zone. The reality was quite different. A couple of blocks were sealed off in downtown Athens, but the rest of the city was bustling, with many people hailing the drastic policy changes as something they were looking forward to. Speaking to a nurse in a state-owned hospital, whose wages would doubtless be lowered, I was surprised to hear the hopeful tone in her voice: "We have been living

> Cities and countries can generate a new sense of cohesion and durability by withstanding hardship and turbulence

unsustainably for a long time … what happens now will change Greece for the better."[6] This sentiment was echoed in many other conversations I had, regardless of whether the person I was speaking to was a state-employed worker or a millionaire entrepreneur, who had most likely been a tax cheat in the years leading up to the meltdown.

The contrast between the images shown by global news outlets and the reality on the streets reminded me of many other trips in the past decade. When the Baltic countries were facing economic disaster in 2009, I was invited as a keynote speaker to a business plan competition for students at a university in Riga. Expecting gloom and disillusionment, I was swept off my feet by the can-do spirit of the students. Instead of sighing in resignation, they used expressions like "we will change Latvia" and "it's time to rebuild". In Dubai in late 2009, I participated in a conference about trends where I had a chance to meet local bankers and entrepreneurs from around the Middle East. While media stories around the world had taken turns to laugh at the many foolish building projects in the emirate, with a not-so-subtle "told you so" attitude after the state-owned development company had defaulted on its extensive debt, the people I met had a pragmatic approach to the whole affair. After all, it wasn't a question of an earthquake wiping Dubai off the map, but of a change of ownership due to an overleveraged model of building. In Manhattan a few weeks after the atrocities of 9/11, I encountered a warm, friendly city where strangers were pulling together and welcoming all visitors as if they were part of one big family. When *The Economist* studied the effects of exogenous events on economies, it found the same kind of resiliency:

Resilience = bouncebackability

The attacks of September 11th, which had an understandable impact on confidence, caused American output to dip by only 0.3% in the third quarter of 2001 … [Unexpected events like the airline-crippling volcanic eruption in April 2010] have very little impact on the global economy. In this, it follows a long line of travel scares that have included SARS, swine flu and terrorist attacks … [Furthermore,] economies are adaptable. Substitution effects predominate. If all air travel were stopped for a year, northern Europeans would no longer make their pilgrimages to Spain and Greece. But they would still take their holidays at home, just as they did before the era of cheap flights: domestic hotels and restaurants would benefit.[7]

A similar kind of bouncebackability can be seen in the fluctuation of the oil price in the 2000s in Figure 8 on the next page. The sudden leap to $147 per barrel and the free-fall drop to $37 in 2008/09 were indeed spectacular, but the overall trend hardly budged, since we can draw quite a smooth linear curve pointing upwards over the course of the decade.

The lesson of these disparate occurrences of resilience is not that communities should be forced to endure unexpected things. We can only imagine the destruction wrought in places like post-earthquake Haiti. Nevertheless, if unexpected things are a naturally occurring part of life – for better or worse – is it not better to focus on the good that these events bring than on the images of despair that media channels insist on placing before us?

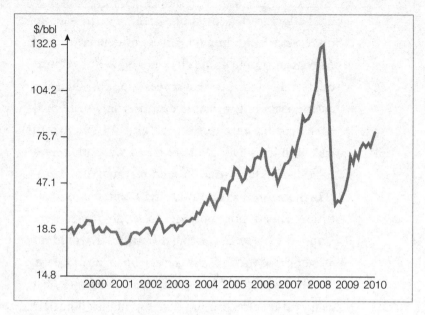

Fig 8 ● Crude oil, average spot price, 2000–10

Source: Bloomberg

◖◗ Anastrophes

How come most people are familiar with the word catastrophe but not its antithesis?

An *anastrophe* is when something unexpected strikes quickly and leaves many people better off than they were

> An anastrophe is when something unexpected strikes quickly and leaves many people better off than they were before

before. One example is the so-called Green Revolution in the mid-twentieth century, an agricultural shift whereby many millions of people in developing nations were lifted out of poverty and starvation.

Another example is the rise of the World Wide Web,

which made information freely accessible to billions and whose creator, Tim Berners-Lee, was nominated for the Nobel Peace Prize in 2010.

These tales make for poor news footage but explain a lot more about human development than the temporary blips caused by strikes, natural disasters or terrorist attacks. What they have in common with these events, however, is that they were unexpected before they occurred. Imagining computer use in the 1980s was to imagine computers on desks being used independently like a bunch of electronic typewriters. The dystopian prophecies of philosophers like Thomas Malthus – wherein population growth outnumbers resources and forces society to return to subsistence conditions – rarely take innovation into account because it is unexpected. Spreading rumours about the imminent demise of mankind if we don't change our habits, invent new engines or start eating in new ways may even speed up the process of invention.

We need someone to make our decisions for us and take a wider perspective on life, society and the future

Add to this the fact that many people want to be led. We need someone to make our decisions for us – a chief executive or prime minister – and take a wider perspective on life, society and the future. For leaders to adapt to an unpredictable world, they would have to use the three dreaded words "I don't know" a lot more. This is unlikely. Do we want ambivalent leaders? Most likely not, but what we get instead are leaders who sometimes give the illusion of control and make erroneous judgements built on faulty analysis, whereas an "I don't know" would have better served society's or the company's wellbeing. The next chapter will focus on what happens when people hijack the unexpected to further their own agenda.

Chapter 4 – The Game

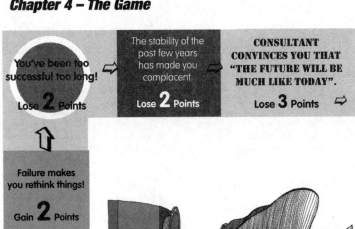

You've been too successful! too long!

Lose 2 Points

The stability of the past few years has made you complacent.

Lose 2 Points

CONSULTANT CONVINCES YOU THAT "THE FUTURE WILL BE MUCH LIKE TODAY".

Lose 3 Points

Failure makes you rethink things!

Gain 2 Points

CHANCE ENCOUNTER MAKES YOU **fall in love.**

Gain 3 Points

You rely too much on a linear process.

Lose 1 Point

5. The telephone as radio

One early idea was to market the phone as a way of listening to live music. Can't make it to the concert hall? Just dial up and listen through the receiver. The idea failed to catch on, but people weren't slow to see another potential use of the invention.

The last ten books you read were recommended by like-minded friends.

Lose 2 Points

CAUTION, Beware of invisible creatures!

Gain 1 Point

You are fired from work.

Gain 3 Points

5 The bad side

The people who hijack and exploit the unexpected

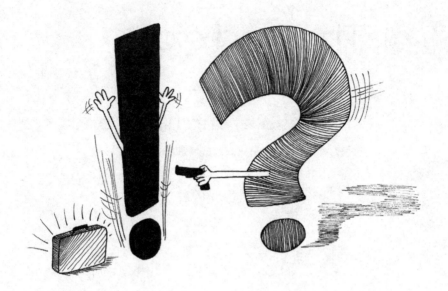

> "You can mispredict things your entire life and still think you can get it right the next time"
>
> Nassim Nicholas Taleb

◖ The dream machine

In the summer of 2008, I attended a morning seminar in Stockholm hosted by an American futurist. The theme was "What lies ahead", and the invitation had promised "deep insights into the unknown world of tomorrow". The futurist was a typical, middle-aged American male with an uncanny resemblance to the celebrity psychologist Dr Phil. His demeanour was that of a well-travelled, knowledgeable expert in his field. He even headed an "institute", a title which, although non-proprietary, lends an air of credibility to an organization. Futurist Dr Phil began by outlining the biggest challenges in the world today, featuring all the usual suspects: climate change, financial market meltdown, the end of oil and China turning belligerent (one reason given for this was the cadre of Chinese bachelors unable to find a wife in China because of the one-child-per-family policy). He kept on saying things like "we are entering an area we've never seen before" or "unimaginable change" for dramatic effect. His conclusion was that "the entire system that we're basing the world on right now" would collapse. Finance, oil, and many other things were all going out of the window because "they did not work". This rather drastic conclusion was followed by a prediction that we're entering a new age "where even mankind might evolve into a new being". When his assumptions were challenged, he just smirked and gave a kind of "if you have to ask you would not understand it anyway" answer.

His presentation was building up to a denouement of sorts. He paused, lowered his voice just in case we were being wiretapped and introduced his institute's invention, "The Dream Machine". The technology, which the institute was supposedly "refusing to sell to the US government although they want it", was based on the assumption ("assumption" as in "vague guess") that people tend to "dream more vivid dreams prior to big tragedies like the tsunami and 9/11". If we could hook all these people up to a machine, they could talk about their dreams and intuitions "before the events happen". A prediction machine, in other words. A machine capable of looking into the future.

Whoa!

Eh?

His friend had already used the machine and predicted that "by 2012, everything will look different".

Apart from the goofiness of this futurist, alarming and amusing in equal measures, the more worrying aspect of this seminar was the amount of nodding and "oh yes" that went on among the participants.

Doomsaying, quasi-scientific conspiracy theorists may be amusing to listen to in small doses but when they start masquerading as "professors", "futurists" and "consultants", they may actually do some harm. Unfortunately, society is full of these shamans hawking everything from cancer cures to business strategy and political dilemmas. This chapter will focus on why these kinds of dubious manipulators flourish in times of uncertainty and why their message resonates so well with many people.

◗ The fog of the future

If life is a highway, the road ahead is shrouded in deep fog concealing whatever lies around the next bend. London Business School professor Don Sull has coined the term "the Fog of the Future" to describe the landscape in which corporate executives and policymakers have to manoeuvre. The fog, in turn, creates fear as we imagine all kinds of horrors lurking in the dense white mist ahead. "Unknown unknowns" tap into our collective psyche and dig out whatever it is we fear the most, not because these things are the most likely to happen but because they best represent

> If life is a highway, the road ahead is shrouded in deep fog concealing whatever lies around the next bend

our view of how the world works – a kind of Rorschach test, if you will. Every historical era stares into a void and sees mysterious beings staring back. In the late nineteenth century, when people imagined aliens, they saw gnomes and trolls, whereas we tend to see aliens as somewhat superior beings – benevolent gods or vicious killing machines. Similarly, the big threat of the 1960s was a nuclear missile attack by a superpower, while the most commonly envisioned scenario today is a terrorist cell using a dirty bomb to wreak havoc on some freedom-loving city.

Interviewing executives at a global media conglomerate, I became aware of the power that the unknown wields: "We live in constant fear that somebody like Google will come along and trounce our entire business. The unknown enemy is very scary."[1]

That fear is a product of the unknown is a truism of sorts, yet few of us stop and ask ourselves why. The reason is actually quite simple. The unknown is hijacked by witch doctors – be it in medicine, science, business or politics – who exploit our fear and greed respectively. These two driving forces can be used to understand everything from management literature ("How to excel in business") and newspaper headlines ("Thousands could die") to lottery advertisements ("It could happen to you") and doomsday cults ("The end is nigh").

◖◗ Merchants of doubt

The currency witch doctors use is extensive airing of questions like "why?" and "what if?" The product they sell is doubt, and business is booming. The reason is that doubt virtually sells itself. Certainty requires either belief or extensive research efforts, while doubt only asks that we hesitate and treat everything that "they" tell us with a little scepticism. While a basic level of doubt is a healthy feature of society, it is especially rife in times of great change, when old power structures crumble and new ones scramble to take their place. To a certain extent, doubt is a sign of fresh thinking. All progress starts by asking questions,

All progress starts by asking questions

but when it comes to exploiting people's relationship with the unknown, sowing doubt can be seen as counterproductive to the pursuit of enlightenment that drives scientific discovery and societal advancement. Making us fear cancer because we don't know exactly when or whom it will strike does nothing for our ability to prevent and cure it. Scaring us with worst-case scenarios about the financial market or the consequences of globalization doesn't help us understand it. Like mental masturbation, scaremongering and scepticism are simply exercises in emotional sensationalism that sometimes masquerade as intellectual theory. So why are they so successful? Partly because negative thoughts will always affect us on a deeper level than optimism, and partly because people inherently need to feel that the times they live in are special, even unique.

> People inherently need to feel that the times they live in are special

> Scaremongering and scepticism are simply exercises in emotional sensationalism

◖◗ The most dangerous world ... ever

Figure 9 on the next page was created by the Centre for Research on the Epidemiology of Disasters, whose findings are alarming. We've never had as many disasters, natural and man-made, in the world as in the past decade, and it seems as if more people are dying as a consequence of them.

This line of argument is familiar to avid newspaper

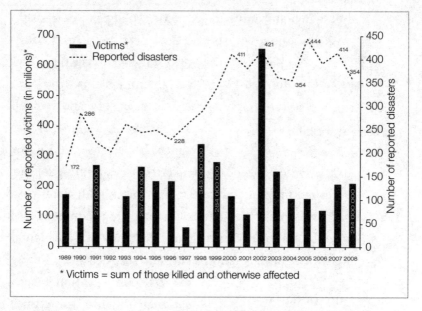

Fig 9 ● Reported disasters, 1989–2008 (occurrence and victims)
Source: Centre for Research on the Epidemiology of Disasters

readers or attendees of NGO-hosted seminars about the world's many ills and ailments. "We live in a unique period in history and most things seem to be getting worse." "We have never faced challenges like these before." And so on. Throughout history, people have always sought to glorify or vilify the present using any means possible, preferably statistics. Most of these statements are quite easy to disprove. Look again at the figure above. The graph shows the number of reported disasters, and while our eyes fix on the second word, it is the first one that makes all the difference. *Reported* disasters. Is it any wonder that the number of reported disasters has increased in the past decade, when information technology has exploded in use, reach and accessibility? With television cameras and Internet access ubiquitous across the globe, we would expect the number of reports about virtually anything to increase. Earthquakes or mass killings in desolate areas that would once have remained in the dark now become headline news the same day. The term "report" is quite a clinical one for what happens.

Blaming the media for increased alarmism is like accusing food of making us fat

When the media lens sweeps across a landscape devastated by a flood, a hurricane or the depredations of a military junta, words like "dramatize" better describe what the journalists are doing. This is sometimes necessary in order to stir the morning newspaper reader from his or her morning slumber, but when dramatization and speculation trounce objective observation, media become a tool of deception, not clarification.

Take Figure 10 on the next page as an example. It shows a number of media stories on looming dangers and epidemics, as well as the actual number of casualties in each of the events reported. The number of stories and the number of deaths are completely unrelated. The conclusion is obvious; the media likes to scare us, even though fewer people seem to be affected by what they try to scare us with.

Charts like these can easily make us believe that the media is to blame for misleading the masses, and that they are as guilty as any other witch doctor of exploiting the unexpected. Blaming the media for increased alarmism, however, is like accusing food of making us fat. The media is a product created to meet our needs. If people wanted to

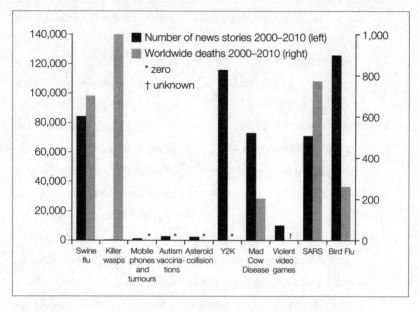

Fig 10 ● Number of media stories about various headlines, 2000–10, and actual deaths caused

Source: Informationisbeautiful.net

digest statistical reports and arcane doctoral theses with their morning coffee, that is what they would get. People are not fact-driven but story-driven. Most of us prefer an emotionally resonant piece of storytelling to a dull, complex presentation of facts. Witch doctors exist not because of some inherent evil but because we often like what it is they are selling and titillating us with. Furthermore, media stories aren't just made up to scare us; there *are* some things in the world that actually make it a more "dangerous" place, if by danger we mean that more people are put at risk.

● *More people in more cities*: There have never been more people on earth than now, and in 2007 the urban population overtook the number of rural inhabitants.[2] We also earn more money than our historical peers. These three factors conspire to create a world where death tolls rise, economic damage is unparalleled and more people are at risk of geographically confined events such as terrorist attacks or earthquakes. The absolute figures presented in the media need to be seen in a historical context, however, and calculated in relative terms, if we are to understand actual as opposed to perceived risk.

- *Connected by fragility*: We live in a world where small things can have a big impact. When two guys get together and create a new search engine, society prospers, but when five guys get together to plan a terrorist attack, society is in peril. When flying is cheaper than taking a taxi, we should expect citizens from all over the world to be present and at risk of being victims whenever something bad happens – be it the terrorist strikes in Bali or the Indian Ocean tsunami. The fact that more people are more easily affected is not necessarily evidence of a more dangerous world, but it creates instability. When a couple of cartoons in a Danish newspaper become a big issue in the Middle East, we are quite obviously dealing with forces far more potent than what we saw a century ago.

  Everything from the school system to corporate budgeting rests upon the assumption that tomorrow will be somewhat similar to today

- *The Anxiety Gap*: Think again of the exponentially sloping Ketchup Effect and compare it to the linear

way in which human beings learn and plan ahead.
Everything from the school system to corporate
budgeting rests upon the assumption that tomorrow will
be somewhat similar to today. We go to primary school,
then secondary school, and so on. Companies plan to
increase costs by 8.9 per cent. And so forth. When the
Ketchup Effect strikes, a gap emerges – between our
way of thinking and reality's way of behaving. When
people say that the world is moving too quickly, it is this
Anxiety Gap they are describing. When we feel that the
world is becoming a more dangerous place, it is because
our mental models for understanding it are out of sync
with the new ways in which it functions.

◖◗ Hijackers of the unexpected

Exploiters of the unexpected seldom care about such
trivial matters as fact or reality, however. What they aim
for is our patternicity – the human instinct to find narrative threads, described in Chapter 2 – and our lack of
knowledge. By filling this void with seductively simplistic
explanations, witch doctors fulfil a deep-seated human
need. Simplicity is the key to successful manipulation of
the human psyche. Reality is often complex, and explain-
ing it from a scientific perspective usually entails lengthy
research with vague or ambivalent conclusions. Better,
then, to find simple, easy-to-understand explanations to
make sense of the puzzle.

This is the foundation on which conspiracy theories
("It was the government") and denialism ("Vaccines
create autism") rest. We don't have to roam the extreme

outskirts of society to find examples, though. If you watch an episode of *Mad Men*, a television drama set in the world of a 1960s advertising agency, you find that

Simplicity is the key to successful manipulation of the human psyche

clients were easily duped by charismatic arguments in an age before metrics and measurable effects. Similarly, business gurus and motivational speakers often attribute success to only seven factors or fewer. Fundamentalist religion reduces everything to one simple factor: not living in accordance with God.

A mindset like this is destructive. Instead of scientifically scrutinizing claims and phenomena, entire societies become mired in poverty and superstition. Take the following quote from Wilbert, a teacher in Haiti, about the desperate conditions the Haitians had to face even before the 2010 earthquake: "I think the Haitian people have been made to suffer by God but the time will come soon when we will be rewarded with Heaven."[3] To this, one can only add, laconically, the words of French designer Philippe Starck: "God becomes the reason when we don't know the reason."[4]

Another way of exploiting the murky waters where the unknown meets the unexpected is typified by the many alarmist groups that have risen up since the fears of climate change re-emerged in the early 2000s. An example of this could be seen when a cyclone caused widespread destruction in India and Bangladesh in May 2009. At a time when efforts should have been focused on immediate emergency relief, Greenpeace used the catastrophe to push its own agenda: "India must continue to pressure the industrialized world to make deep and urgent cuts in greenhouse gas emissions,"[5] a press release stated. It was hardly surprising. Only a few years earlier, influential environmental NGO the Sierra Club urged members to "ride the wave of public concern created over extreme weather".[6]

A certain degree of gloom may act as a healthy reminder of actual underlying problems. It becomes problematic when the discussions unravel into emotionally charged mudslinging instead of sober, intellectual inquiry. Too many complicated issues – from the science of climate change to the boundaries of religious freedom – become mired in ideological shouting matches that bring us no closer to possible solutions.

The consequences of hijackers in the world of business may be less severe than the oppression and suffering of many societies, but they are no less prevalent. Business professor Phil Rosenzweig has written about the so-called Halo Effect, whereby companies are at first admired and put on a pedestal, complete with a halo, only to be dethroned in the next instant and criticized for whatever it is they do. We see this happening whenever a company or brand luxuriates in the hype and frenzy of mainstream fame only to be dumped like yesterday's garbage when something new and exciting comes along. Microsoft, ABB and Nike are but a few examples.

◗ The *Titanic* was unsinkable

The risk posed by these witch doctors is that they often go beyond influencing discussion and focus on setting policy and urging action. Human beings have a deep-seated propensity to act. That is, we are reluctant to wait and see whenever something dramatic unfolds before us and we would much rather do anything rather than regret doing nothing. This can have disas-trous consequences on both an individual and a broader basis. An example of the former is the tragic death of Swedish Formula One star Ronnie Peterson, who died an untimely death after crashing his racing car in 1978. Calling deaths in a highly dangerous sport tragic might seem like an overstatement, but Peterson died not of the collision itself but of the doctors' decision to operate quickly. With mul-tiple fractures in his legs, the operation caused small bone fragments to break off and lodge in his brain. Peterson was declared dead later that day. The common procedure nowadays is for patients with multiple fractures to be sedated so that the body can rest and heal itself. Doing nothing might, in other words, have saved Ronnie Peter-son's life.

> We would much rather do anything rather than regret doing nothing

Another example is that of the unsinkable *Titanic*, whose fate has become a legend, not least because the claim "unsinkable" was so audacious and became a mani-festation of human hubris. The irony is that the *Titanic was* in a sense unsinkable. The many chambers in its hull would have protected the ship from a collision far more potent than that with the iceberg on 15 April 1912 *if* it had been a head-on collision. The crew of the *Titanic* famously manoeuvred to the port side of the iceberg, which tore a hole in the side that ultimately sank the ship. The ship was built to withstand collisions, but not the human tendency to act in unpredictable, sometimes devastating, ways. These examples matter because it has become somewhat fashionable for politicians to use the word "unexpected" as a kind of argument for making decisions or protecting themselves from public furore. After all, what is the war on terror if not a war on unexpected events?

The leadership delusion

People's willingness to listen to the junk science, conspiracy theories and random assaults of witch doctors has its roots in the gap between our search for meaning and the perceived meaninglessness of many events that affect our daily lives. The many sides of the unexpected described in this book – be they disruptive innovations or ghastly catastrophes – have in common that they just happen. They are neither signs of divine intervention nor easily explained by the casual relationships journalists want to portray. They strike without people having done anything wrong, which may seem unfair to industries shaken up by a groundbreaking invention or the thousands displaced by a sudden landslide. We look for people who might explain the meaningless. Some argue that doing so is the very essence of leadership. We need leaders not just to make decisions but also to make sense. Take what is random and make it meaningful.

We need leaders not just to make decisions but also to make sense

Unfortunately, leadership can generate overconfidence in single individuals, which incapacitates individual judgement and critical thinking. I encountered this in the summer of 2008 when I was consulting for a large bank. The financial sector had started to shake badly that spring, and its volatility had now reached feverish proportions. The bank I worked with had just discovered significant credit losses and the CEO had been fired. My client, whom I had worked with for the past few months to create a forward-thinking programme for top executives, put it as follows: "You cannot underestimate how bad the situation has become. When we start working together again after the summer break, we can't be as optimistic about the future as we were in the spring sessions." Not wanting to let him down, I invested significant effort in crafting a highly pessimistic outlook to be presented to a group of senior executives a few weeks later. They hated it. Not just what I said but the way I said it. "Has he even prepared?" was a question that came back to me in the feedback questionnaire. I was dumbfounded, but my contact filled me in. "You see, Magnus, we had the new CEO here yesterday and he told us that the problems we faced had been overestimated and taken out of proportion. We will be fine. Everything is under control." Two weeks later, the bank filed for bankruptcy.

What this and other well-known examples of delusional leadership show are that the seductive calm of a leader can easily lead us astray. The bank that I worked for was perhaps doomed even as the CEO addressed them, and there was little that the executives could have done to change course in the company's

The seductive calm of a leader can easily lead us astray

last few weeks. But situations like these are replicated every day around the world, with leaders expecting a nod and a "yes!" while dissenters are called names, ostracized or even fired.

Learning to live with the unexpected

It's early morning and I let my two-year-old twins entertain themselves with online videos while I make some breakfast. A scream pierces the morning calm and both my twins run away from the computer screen crying. The online video that began with a child-friendly cartoon had suddenly morphed into horrific images of blood and gore. We had been trolled.

Although trolls have been a part of folklore for centuries, it wasn't until recently that they stepped out of fantasy and into the real world. "Troll" is the nickname given to someone who hacks into or vandalizes websites, often with malicious intent. A famous prank entailed hacking into the website of an organization for epileptics and making the home page flash like a stroboscope. Although not without some finesse, much of what trolls achieve can best be likened to bullying or common antisocial behaviour. It also shares a few traits with those other Ts – terrorists. Both groups are partly motivated by ideology, however weakly defined it may be, and they build their ideas on exploiting human structures and behaviours – from our way of communicating to our way of travelling.

> There is no way of predicting where the combined ideas of billions of people will take us next

They are also examples of human ingenuity gone bad – if by bad we mean that they take lives and cause mental suffering – and herein lies the ultimate reason why the world will continue to be a cesspool of unpredictability for the foreseeable future. To quote Immanuel Kant: "Out of the crooked timber of humanity no straight thing was ever made."

There is no way of predicting where the combined ideas of billions of people will take us next. The twentieth century was about empowering the individual by leaving constrictive institutions behind and giving her access to ever more power tools with which to express herself, be they mass communication or mass destruction. Con-

Constraints do little to inhibit creativity

straints – in the form of denying resources or imposing stricter legislation – do little to inhibit this creativity. In fact, one can argue that constraints even boost creativity. Think about taxes, for example. Where in Europe are you bound to find the most creative tax lawyers? In Andorra, where there are virtually no taxes, or in Sweden, where the tax rate rates are high and viciously enforced? Creativity loves constraints, and by pursuing security we create a kind of paradox. Tightening security forces individuals with malevolent intentions to come up with more creative ways to beat the system – think shoe bombers and underwear made of explosives. Security may sometimes cause the very problems it is put in place to prevent, and it also leads to a world that is more, not less, unpredictable.

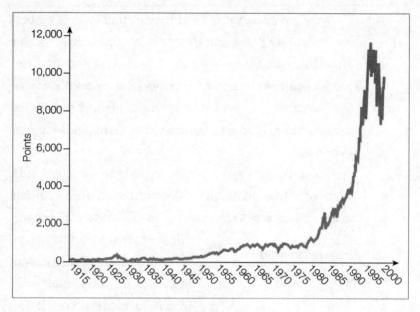

Fig 11 ● The Dow Jones Industrial Average, 1916–2002

Source: Benoit Mandelbrot

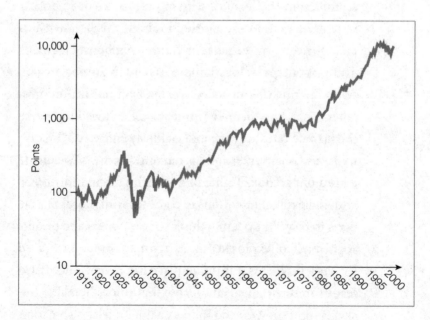

Fig 12 ● The Dow in logarithmic scale, 1912–2002

Source: Benoit Mandelbrot

◖ Just say no!

On the whole, increased creativity and individual ideas are something to celebrate. In the rare instances where they destabilize and cause suffering, we should be wary of drawing quick conclusions. There are no upsides without downsides, and if we want to live in a world where people are free to create whatever they want, we must accept that some of this creativity will be destructive. The real enemy is not human ingenuity but the hordes of hijacking witch doctors who abuse unpredictability to push their own agenda. That is when you and I have a duty to say "No more! Don't use your scare tactics on us!" That is how the Age of Enlightenment began. As quacks on the streets of Lisbon started selling anti-earthquake medicine in the aftermath of the great earthquake of 1755, philosophers and scientists created a backlash that in turn gave birth to new scientific discoveries and societies built on rational insight, not superstition. Fear is a poor guide to the future, and even worse as a trigger for decision-making.

Fear is a poor guide to the future

It may be refreshing, then, to consider the following. If you look at a chart illustrating stock market performance over the past century (Figure 11), it will indeed seem as if the world market is spinning out of control. A drastic and volatile increase like this surely cannot last.

But let us look at this from another perspective. If we rescale the chart logarithmically (Figure 12), "it makes the charts look the way the market actually felt to someone who was living through it".[7] Gone is the drastic upswing that made the past decade seem like something historically unparalleled, and in its place we see a world where growth is slow but steady and where some days are better than others.

In the words of author Bruce Sterling: "We may be on the edge of nothing particularly important."[8]

Chapter 5 – The Game

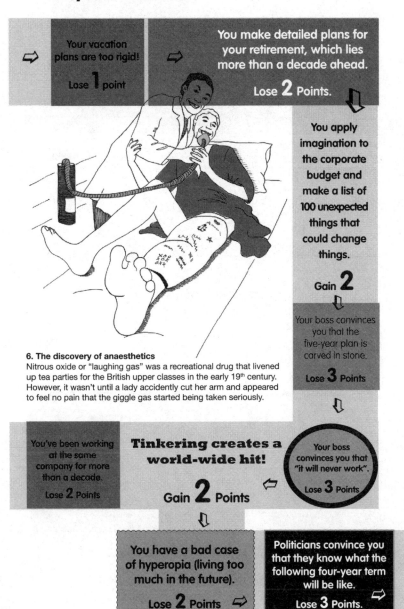

⇨ Your vacation plans are too rigid!

Lose **1** point

⇨ You make detailed plans for your retirement, which lies more than a decade ahead.

Lose **2** Points.

⇩ You apply imagination to the corporate budget and make a list of 100 unexpected things that could change things.

Gain **2**

⇩ Your boss convinces you that the five-year plan is carved in stone.

Lose **3** Points

⇩

6. The discovery of anaesthetics
Nitrous oxide or "laughing gas" was a recreational drug that livened up tea parties for the British upper classes in the early 19th century. However, it wasn't until a lady accidently cut her arm and appeared to feel no pain that the giggle gas started being taken seriously.

You've been working at the same company for more than a decade.

Lose **2** Points

Tinkering creates a world-wide hit!

Gain **2** Points

Your boss convinces you that "it will never work".

Lose **3** Points

⇩

You have a bad case of hyperopia (living too much in the future).

Lose **2** Points ⇨

Politicians convince you that they know what the following four-year term will be like.

Lose **3** Points. ⇨

6 Conclusion: A bright, uncertain future

Adapting to and enjoying life in an unpredictable world

"Live in fragments no longer. Only connect ..."

E. M. Forster, *Howards End*, 1910

A day without surprises

Seven a.m. Monday morning. Your alarm clock rings. You press "snooze". What's the point of getting up?

This is the day without surprises. For some reason, you have been given a script for how everything will be played out in the coming twenty-four hours. It's all there. The events. The people you meet. Big things as well as minute details. Your thoughts. Your feelings.

Your initial excitement at reading this slowly gives way to a draining feeling of emptiness as the thrill of surprise is replaced by ... well, nothing.

There are plenty of reasons to dread the unexpected, but ask yourself whether you would really trade the nasty surprises that strike us every now and then for a lifetime of knowing exactly what lay ahead. A certain future would most likely make us chronically depressed. The delight of surprises and the enchanting mystery we call the future are essential ingredients in happiness. If that were not the case, prison inmates serving life sentences would be the happiest people on earth.

◖◗ The beauty of the unexpected

This book began with a series of unexpected events that had scared us – from natural disasters to man-made ones – but went on to show that the unexpected can be a source of many good things – from pleasant surprises to ground-breaking new innovations. The unexpected is a benevolent force capable of making us think new thoughts, create new ideas and challenge stale assumptions. It powers creativity, science, personal development and societal progress. Even bad events can lead to a better tomorrow as safety measures improve and we are forced to find new ways of solving problems.

> The unexpected is a benevolent force capable of making us think new thoughts

A recent book title captured this well: *The Alchemy of Growth*. Growth, whether it is personal or in business and society, makes something out of nothing, just like an alchemist does, and its secret ingredient is the unexpected. Before inventions happen, it is often assumed that what they provide cannot be achieved. In an interview, the vice-president of innovation at a large multinational, a man credited with inventing Wi-Fi, explained his success as an innovator in the following way: "There were at least twenty academic papers saying that Wi-Fi would never work in reality. I decided that they must be wrong and set about finding a solution." Out of nothing came something. That is the alchemic nature of growth. It is repeated not just in the world of business but in popular culture, politics and societal progress. From the rise of pop-culture phenomena like Dan Brown and Coldplay to the fall of dictatorships. The unexpected is always looming somewhere at the heart of these events. The unexpected is life.

The age of uncertainty

Some argue that information technology will slowly phase out the elements of unpredictability, as powerful processors will be able to quickly process all kinds of information and accurately predict every outcome imaginable. IT conferences and branding campaigns around the world talk about the shift from "guessing" to "knowing". Technology magazine *Wired* even went as far as heralding the death of science itself. With the rise of petabyte computers, the magazine argued, hypotheses can be formulated and answered in real time, eliminating the need for the uncertain, drawn-out tests on which science relies. Similar arguments are made about risk management ("Computers will be able to accurately predict everything that can possibly go wrong") as well as the future of media consumption ("Algorithms will predict what movies you will enjoy, eliminating the need for critics").

> What might seem extraordinary to us may seem like a walk in the park for our children

What futuristic scenarios like these – thrilling as they may be – fail to take into account is the elusive nature of the unexpected. Like the boundaries of the human mind, the unexpected's boundaries keep moving simply because it is a figment of our imagination. A word invented by man to serve our needs. What we expect in life shifts between individuals and generations. What might seem extraordinary to us may seem like a walk in the park for our children. Consider what "an act of terrorism" or "stock market volatility" meant to previous generations and compare this to how they are perceived today. The human brain has a relentless need to see patterns, find narratives and meaning. Until evolution sends it in some unexpected new direction, this is unlikely to change.

What does change is our relationship to uncertainty, and I would argue that we are more comfortable with it than ever. Consider the meaning of life itself. We used to live in a world where meaning was pre-packaged for us, and we would have little room to challenge the doctrines laid out by holy texts or the shackles of a rigid, patriarchal class system. When social commentators sometimes bemoan the lack of meaning in modern society, one can only hope that they don't want to see a return to the constrictive, oppressive top-down pecking order of yesterday. Today, there is no meaning, and most societies around the world teach their young to go out and find it for themselves: in a steady stream of action, thoughts and things happening, it's up to me to put these things together to find meaning. A metaphor and a simile come to mind when describing this shift. The metaphor is a road that used to be straight and lined with instructive street signs. Today, it is a foggy serpentine track bordered by a spectacular yet occasionally perilous landscape. The simile is based on literary genres. The old way of creating meaning can be likened to most bestselling novels; a straight narrative, linear and unambiguous in plot. The new way of creating meaning is like poetry; open to many different interpretations.

◑ Thriving in a poem

In the winter of 2002, *The Economist* ran an essay competition along with the Shell oil company. The question asked was "How much freedom should we give up for our security?" – a popular question in the aftermath of the 9/11 terrorist attacks. This question is not new, and many philosophers have had their say on the matter – Baron Montesquieu's "Freedom is to do whatever the law permits" comes to mind. The winning essay was quite remarkable. Minnesota resident Jack Gordon seemed at first to digress completely by talking about his beloved sailing excursions on Lake Superior, but used these to draw a poignant analogy:

> Safety is a fine thing, but as an obsession it rots
> the soul. If I should live to be ninety, and I am
> called upon to attest to the other nursing-home
> residents that my life was about something racier
> than guessing right on the butter-vs-margarine
> conundrum, I will speak of that thunderstorm
> on Lake Superior. I'll describe the touch-and-go
> struggle to keep the boat pointed just enough
> off the wind to maintain headway, and the
> jackhammer pounding of a madly luffing mainsail
> trying to spill a 75-knot gale. I'll talk about the way
> we huddled in the cockpit with our eyes rigidly
> forward because looking aft would mean another
> lightning-illuminated glimpse of the dinghy we

towed, risen completely out of the water and twirling like a propeller on the end of its line.

Pleasant though many of them were, with the cheese and crackers and such, I doubt I'll have much to say about the hours I spent on Superior with the sails furled, motoring in perfect safety through flat water and dead air.[1]

There are many different ways to interpret what has happened in the world in the past decade, and we have seen in the previous chapter how many choose to portray every norm-deviating event as evidence of a race to the bottom for humanity. What Gordon's essay and this book urge us to do is to reclaim uncertainty from the jaws of fear and install it firmly as the centrepiece of life. Life is about taking chances and risks, and they would not be called "risks" if there weren't a potential downside. Astronaut John Glenn famously put it the following way moments before blast-off: "Oh my God, I'm sitting on a pile of low bids."

Chapter 6 – The Game

Massive Attack of the Unexpected.

Gain **3** Points!

⇧   ⇩

Shaman convinces you that it's all fate.

Lose **3** Points

⇧   ⇩

7. The world's biggest photo album

Ludicorp had a clear vision: to build the world's biggest multiplayer online game. But there was a problem. Players wanted to communicate more visually, so a quick and easy tool was developed for photo hosting. Then there was another problem. People started sharing photos more than playing the game. Flickr now contains more than 4 billion images worldwide.

You decide to get lost.

Gain **2** Points

⇧   ⇩

You try combining two separate ideas and an invention is born.

Gain **3** Points

⇧

⇨

You decide to practise everything this book says.

Gain **10** Points

⇨

Surprise drought.

Lose **2** Points

⇩

Randomness scares you.

Lose **1** Point

⇧

Congratulations, you stumble upon six new insights in a day.

⇨ Gain **2** Points

Success!
Enlightenment and a newly-found trust in the unexpected.

Epilogue:
Rebirth

"It all changed in an instant"

six-word memoir by Candis Sykes

I'm on board a Finnair Airbus A340 jet about to land in Hong Kong. It is July 2009 and a nasty hurricane has moved in over the city. The aircraft jolts violently from side to side. I grip the armrests feverishly and clench my jaws. Having had a fear of flying since I was a teenager, I especially dread turbulence, even when it's mild. This is severe. And getting worse.

The captain comes on the PA to warn anyone against leaving his or her seat, as we are about to fly through a thunderstorm. I am slowly moving from a state of terror to the calm of knowing that this is the end. Slowly, the terror loses its grip on me and is replaced by a state of calm. I am certain that these are my final moments on earth and a sense of tranquillity overcomes me. I listen to the thunderbolts as they vigorously shake the fuselage in all directions. I close my eyes and glide along with the plane's erratic path. I'm not afraid any more. I feel my hands gripping the armrest and I slowly unclench them and turn my palms upwards instead. What a feeling of bliss. It's as if I'm now a surfer with the plane as my board and the sky as my waves. The future can take me where it wants to.

I am not afraid any more.

I am not afraid.

Thank you!

Martin Liu for making me an author.

Simon Benham for being my agent.

My wife Vesna for her relentless and heartfelt support, no matter what the circumstance.

Gustav for adding the element of surprise to the illustrations.

Peter for trawling the neurological depths of the unexpected.

Ola, Joakim, Jörgen, Tobias and Fredrik for being my test subjects.

Robin – "*Mens sana in corpore sano.*"

And finally to Nassim Nicholas Taleb, whose sharp intellect enlightened me and whose boundless arrogance gave me my path.

Notes

Chapter 1

1   H. Frank Knight, *Risk, Uncertainty and Profit*, Signalman Publishing, Orlando, 2009.

2   Michael Shermer, "The pattern behind self-deception", TED talk, Long Beach, CA, 10 February 2010, http://www.youtube.com/watch?v=b_6-iVz1Roo, accessed 2 May 2010.

3   Michael Shermer, "Patternicity: finding meaningful patterns in meaningless noise", *Scientific American*, December 2008, http://www.scientificamerican.com/article.cfm?id=patternicity-finding-meaningful-patterns, accessed 1 December 2009.

4   Arlea Æðelwyrd Hunt-Anschütz, "What is Wyrdwords", *Cup of Wonder*, October 2001, http://www.wyrdwords.vispa.com/heathenry/whatwyrd.html, accessed 2 October 2009.

5   Niall Ferguson, "Sun could set suddenly on superpower as debt bites", *Real Clear World*, 10 July 2010, http://www.realclearworld.com/articles/2010/07/28/sun_could_set_suddenly_on_superpower_as_debt_bites_99088.html, accessed 24 September 2010.

6   Personal interview, member of the Swedish armed forces (name withheld at request of interviewee). Conducted in Stockholm on 27 January 2010.

7   Charles McGrath, "After Spidey, a return to Hell", *New York Times*, 21 May 2009, http://www.nytimes.com/2009/05/24/movies/24mcgr.html?pagewanted=2, accessed 21 June 2009.

8   Marty Neumeier, "The brand gap", Slideshare presentation, 2003, http://www.slideshare.net/coolstuff/the-brand-gap, accessed 20 March 2010.

Chapter 2

1   Bryan Oden, "Ringtone", *Innocentenglish*, 2008, http://www.innocentenglish.com/best-funny-jokes/funniest-jokes.html, accessed 2 April 2010.

2   Daniel Elkan, "The comedy circuit", *New Scientist*, 30 January 2010, pp. 40–43.

3   Paul Hinz, "Irishman jokes", *The Definitive Jokes Collection*, http://www.paulhitz.com/college/irish.html, accessed 13 February 2010.

4   TT, "Kejsarsnitt ändrar barns DNA", *Aftonbladet*, 29 June 2009, http://www.aftonbladet.se/wendela/barn/article5444759.ab, accessed 2 May 2010.

5   Radio interview with Tom Lundin, professor of disaster psychiatry, Uppsala University. Broadcast on Swedish Radio P1, 21 September 2009.

6   Dave Cullen, *Columbine*, Old Street Publishing, London, 2009.

7   Maia Szalavitz, "10 ways we get the odds wrong", *Psychology Today*, 1 January 2008, http://www.psychologytoday.com/articles/200712/10-ways-we-get-the-odds-wrong, accessed 2 May 2010.

8   Anna Asker, "Hjärnan gillar repriser", *Svd*, 27 January 2009, http://www.svd.se/nyheter/idagsidan/halsa/hjarnan-gillar-repriser_2381171.svd, accessed 28 April 2010.

9   FT Special Report, "Global brands", *Financial Times*, 5 April 2009, http://www.scribd.com/doc/14942787/FT-special-on-Brandz-Brands-2009, accessed 14 February 2010.

10 Jonah Lehrer, "Accept defeat: the neuroscience of screwing up", *Wired*, 21 December 2009, http://www.wired.com/magazine/2009/12/fail_accept_defeat/2/, accessed 21 January 2010.

11 First sentences quoted exactly as in Benedict Carey, "How nonsense sharpens the intellect", *New York Times*, 5 October 2009, http://www.nytimes.com/2009/10/06/health/06mind.html?_r=2&em, accessed 20 April 2010.

12 Ibid., http://www.nytimes.com/2009/10/06/health/06mind.html?_r=2&em, accessed 2 November 2009.

13 Ibid.

14 Eric Nagourney, "Surprise! Brain likes thrill of unknown", *New York Times*, 17 April 2001.

15 Lev Grossman, "Do we need the iPad? A TIME review", *Time*, 1 April 2010, http://www.time.com/time/business/article/0,8599,1976932-2,00.html, accessed 1 May 2010.

16 *RoxBox*, box set by Roxette, Inclay card texts by Jan Gradvall. Manuscript of texts supplied by Jan Gradvall on 13 May 2010.

17 Jonah Lehrer, "What we know: creation on command", *Seed*, 6 May 2009.

18 Ibid.

19 Louis Menand, "What comes naturally", *New Yorker*, 22 November 2002.

20 Robert Krulwich, "All things considered – why does time fly by as you get older?", *WBUR*, 1 February 2010.

21 Ibid.

22 Barbara Strauch, "How to train the aging brain", *New York Times*, 29 December 2009, http://www.nytimes.com/2010/01/03/education/edlife/03adult-t.html, accessed 19 March 2010.

23 Ibid.

24 Ibid.

Chapter 3

1 John Hagel III, John Seely Brown and Lang Davison, "The Shift Index", www.johnseelybrown.com, Jun 2009, http://www.johnseelybrown.com/shiftindexabstract.pdf, accessed 1 June 2010.

2 IBM, "2010 global CEO study", *IBM*, 18 May 2010, http://www.ibm.com/news/ca/en/2010/05/20/v384864m81427w34.html, accessed 2 February 2010.

3 Personal interview with Lars Bäcksell. Conducted in Jordbro, Stockholm, on 8 April 2010.

4 Robert Friedel, "Serendipity is no accident", *The Kenyon Review*, 2001, http://www.jstor.org/pss/4338198, accessed 1 March 2010.

5 Peter F. Drucker, *Innovation and Entrepreneurship: Practice and principles*, Harper Paperbacks, New York, p. 37.

6 Joan Magretta, "Why business models matter", *Harvard Business Review*, May 2002, http://info.psu.edu.sa/psu/fnm/asalleh/WhyBusModelMatter.pdf, accessed 23 May 2010.

7 Ken Auletta, *Googled: The End of the World As We Know It*, Penguin Press, New York, 2009.

8 Elizabeth Kolbert, "Hosed – is there a quick fix for the climate?", *New Yorker*, 16 November 2009, http://www.newyorker.com/arts/critics/books/2009/11/16/091116crbo_books_kolbert, accessed 1 June 2010.

9 Huw Richards, "Mintzberg's 5 Ps for strategy", *Institute for Manufacturing*, http://www.ifm.eng.cam.ac.uk/dstools/paradigm/5pstrat.html, accessed 17 February 2010.

10 Ron Martin and Peter Sunley, "Paul Krugman's geographical economics and its implications for regional development theory: a

critical assessment", *Economic Geography*, July 1996, http://members.
shaw.ca/compilerpress1/Anno%20Krugman.htm, accessed 23 May
2010.

11   Jane Jacobs, *Economy of Cities*, Vintage, New York, p. 2.

12   Steven Levy, "Ray Ozzie wants to push Microsoft back into startup
mode", *Wired*, 24 November 2008, http://www.wired.com/techbiz/
people/magazine/16–12/ff_ozzie?currentPage=6, accessed 22 March
2010.

13   Drucker, op. cit., p. 34.

14   Don Sull, *Revival of the Fittest: Why Good Companies Go Bad and
How Great Managers Remake Them*, Harvard University Press,
Cambridge, MA.

15   This is called Austin's Law, and was originally developed by the
Gartner Group.

16   "B&O Railroad Museum," Wikipedia, http://en.wikipedia.org/wiki/
B&O_Railroad_Museum, accessed 28 January 2010.

17   Andrew O'Connell, "Roof collapses and other useful interruptions",
Harvard Business Review, January–February 2010, http://hbr.
org/2010/01/roof-collapses-and-other-useful-interruptions/ar/1,
accessed 15 February 2010.

18   Andy Serwer, "Lehman Brothers: A super-hot machine", CNN, 11
April 2006, http://money.cnn.com/2006/04/10/news/companies/
lehmanintro_f500_fortune_041706/, accessed 1 June 2010.

19   "CEO Richard Fuld on Lehman Brothers' evolution from internal
turmoil to teamwork", *Wharton*, 10 January 2007, http://knowledge.
wharton.upenn.edu/article.cfm?articleid=1631, accessed 13 March
2010.

20   Bruce Einhorn, "The 30 most innovation-friendly countries",
Plazabridge Group, 4 March 2010, http://www.plazabridge.
com/2010/03/04/the-worlds-30-most-innovative-countries/,
accessed 26 March 2010.

21   Sandra Ljung, "Can certainty crush innovation? Norway's curse", *The
Medici Effect*, 21 September 2009, http://www.themedicieffect.com/
uncategorized/can-certainty-crush-innovation-norway's-curse/,
accessed 22 April 2010.

22   Jeffrey Veen, "Jimmy Wales: steak knives and human knowledge",
Ween, 19 April 2006, http://www.veen.com/jeff/archives/000880.
html, accessed 1 May 2010.

23 "Rum remark wins Rumsfeld an award", BBC News, 2 December 2003, http://news.bbc.co.uk/2/hi/3254852.stm, accessed 1 June 2010.

24 Speech by Steven Barnett at the Pazarlama Zirvesi Conference, Istanbul, 11 December 2009.

25 "A special report on financial risk: Cinderella's moment", *The Economist*, http://www.economist.com/specialreports/displaystory. cfm?story_id=15474145, accessed 1 June 2010.

26 Joshua Margolis et al., *Fritidsresor under Pressure: The First 10 Hours*, Harvard Business School case study, 17 September 2006.

27 "Nestlé: The unrepentant chocolatier", *The Economist*, http:// www.economist.com/displaystory.cfm?story_id=E1_TQSQQJRN, accessed 22 May 2010.

28 Carol Bartz, "Fail Fast Forward: appreciating risk", Stanford, 24 October 2001, http://ecorner.stanford.edu/authorMaterialInfo. html?mid=2, accessed 1 June 2010.

29 "A serious take on Internet game play", podcast radio programme, presented by Entrepreneurial Thought Leaders Series at Stanford University, 28 October 2009, http://ecorner.stanford.edu/ authorMaterialInfo.html?mid=2277, accessed 20 May 2010.

Chapter 4

1 Surfdaddy Orca & R.U. Sirus, "Ray Kurzweil: The h+ interview", *H+Magazine*, 30 December 2009, http://www.hplusmagazine.com/ articles/ai/ray-kurzweil-h-interview, accessed 22 June 2010.

2 Matt Ridley, *The Rational Optimist: How Prosperity Evolves*, Fourth Estate, London, 2010.

3 Ed Regis, "The doomslayer", *Wired*, 5(2), February 1997, http://www. wired.com/wired/archive/5.02/ffsimon_pr.html.

4 Daniel Gilbert, "What you don't know makes you nervous", *New York Times*, 20 May 2009, http://opinionator.blogs.nytimes. com/2009/05/20/what-you-dont-know-makes-you-nervous/, accessed 27 August 2010.

5 "The pleasures and sorrows of work: Alain de Botton in conversation with Paul Holdengräber", online video produced by New York Public Library, 8 June 2009, http://www.nypl.org/audiovideo/ pleasures-and-sorrows-work-alain-de-botton-conversation-paul-holdengraeber, accessed 12 June 2009.

6 Personal interview, Athens, Greece, 13 May 2010.

7   "Buttonwood: Heat and dust", *The Economist*, http://www.economist.com/business-finance/displaystory.cfm?story_id=15955520, accessed 1 May 2010.

Chapter 5

1   Interview with R&D team at Bonnier office, Stockholm, 29 April 2010.

2   "Urbanization", Wikipedia, http://en.wikipedia.org/wiki/Urbanization, accessed 27 August 2010.

3   Alex von Tunzelmann, "Haiti: the land where children eat mud", *Sunday Times*, 17 May 2009.

4   Philippe Starck, "Phillipe Starck thinks deep on design", TED Talk, December 2007, http://www.ted.com/talks/philippe_starck_thinks_deep_on_design.html, accessed 27 August 2010.

5   Bjorn Lomborg, "Cyclones and global warming", *Wall Street Journal*, 22 November 2009.

6   Ibid.

7   Benoit Mandelbrot and Richard L. Hudson, *The Misbehaviour of Markets: A Fractal View of Financial Turbulence*, Basic Books, New York, p. 91.

8   Quotation accessed from collection at http://infinitefuture.org/page/4 on 10 June 2010.

Chapter 6

1   Jack Gordon, "Milksop nation", *Free Republic*, 10 February 2003, http://www.freerepublic.com/focus/f-news/839429/posts, accessed 28 April 2010.